D1418094

UNDERSTANDING YOUR PET:
Pet Care and Humane Concerns

By Michael W. Fox

*Integrative Development of Brain
and Behavior in the Dog*

*The Behavior of Wolves, Dogs
and Related Canids*

Understanding Your Dog

Understanding Your Cat

Concepts in Ethology: Animal and Human Behavior

*Between Animal and Man:
The Key to the Kingdom*

*Understanding Your Pet:
Pet Care and Humane Concerns*

Books for children by Michael W. Fox

The Wolf

Vixie, The Story of a Little Fox

Sundance Coyote

*Ramu and Chennai:
Brothers of the Wild*

Wild Dogs Three

Understanding Your Pet

Pet Care and Humane Concerns

Dr. MICHAEL W. FOX

D.SC., Ph.D., B.Vet.Med.,
M.R.C.V.S.

Director, Institute for
the Study of Animal Problems,
The Humane Society of the U.S.
Washington, D.C.

Coward, McCann & Geoghegan, Inc.
New York

Copyright © 1978 by Michael W. Fox

All rights reserved. This book, or parts thereof, may not be reproduced in any form without permission in writing from the publisher. Published on the same day in Canada by Longman Canada Limited, Toronto.

Library of Congress Cataloging in Publication Data

Fox, Michael W 1937-
   Understanding your pet: pet care and humane concerns

   Bibliography: p.
   Includes index.
   1. Pets. 2. Pets—Behavior. I. Title.
SF413.F69   636.08'87   78-4959
ISBN O-698-10851-5

Printed in the United States of America

For all creatures,
great and small

OCT 29 1984

Contents

Acknowledgments

I wish to thank *Saturday Review* and *Defenders of Wildlife* for permission to reprint chapters 11 and 19, repectively, and gratefully appreciate the consent of *McCalls* magazine to include much of my material from my column *Understanding Your Pet*, which has been incorporated in chapters 3–6, 13, 15, 16, and 18–21.

I owe a special thanks to Ms. Patricia Brehaut Soliman, for her constructive editorial comments and encouragement in completing this work.

Foreword

I have spent most of my life with animals, great and small. At first they were simply my playmates and companions; later my care and love for dogs and cats expanded to include curiosity and concern. I was curious about what made them "tick"—what they felt and thought—and developed a deep concern about their mental and physical health. It was natural, then, with such early attitudes and aspirations, that I should become a veterinarian and animal psychologist—more correctly, an ethologist.

This book explores some of the recent advances in veterinary knowledge, and also provides information about animal and—its necessary adjunct for our purposes—human behavior; much of this behavioral material comes from my own research on cats, dogs, wolves, foxes, and other carnivores. I have set it out here to help pet owners improve their relationships with their pets—understanding, after all, is the key to the animal kingdom. And not surprisingly, since we are all related to some degree in the evolutionary past, the more I have learned about animals, the more aware I have become of my own nature and that of my fellow human beings. One who is close to animals and nature is closer to understanding himself.

Such knowledge may also improve the physical and mental health of our pets. To my mind, the well-being of a child, a pet, or a wild animal depends upon the inner health of, respectively, the parents, the family, or the society or culture. Concerned, then, with relating and *relationship*, this book is for those of us who have pets and in consequence bear the burden of the responsibility for animals as well as relationship with them.

Without understanding, there can be neither full responsibility nor fulfilling relationship. I hope this book will further understanding and contribute significantly to fostering an ethic of reverence for all living creatures, however great or small.

PART I

Cats and Dogs

Greyfriar's Bobby—a memorial in Edinburgh to the loyal dog who guarded his master's grave for fourteen years.

1

The Right Pet for You

ARE YOU A dog or a cat person? Your temperament may influence your choice of a pet or of a particular breed. The way the pet business is growing in sophistication, it may not be long before a prospective owner will be able to take a special personality test to aid in selecting the pet most compatible to him. Too often, though, since animals are generally less flexible and less adaptable than people, it is discovered too late that the pet is incompatible with a particular life style or home environment—a house full of noisy children, for example. Because of this, and because many people find the pet too much work or no longer fun when it grows up, no fewer than 13½ million cats and dogs are destroyed every year in the United States. Knowing what kind of pet to get in the first place will help significantly to decrease this tragic figure, and help, too, to improve your life and the life of your pet.

Our preconceptions about animals can get in the way. For example, many people expect a puppy to grow with little training into an obedient and faithful pet like Lassie. They do not realize that having a pup is a big responsibility. The little animal requires much time, patience, and attention: it cannot be left to its own devices. A dog responds to a leader, and the owner must be prepared for and knowledgeable about this role. Similarly, preconceptions can get in the way of relating to a kitten. Some believe a cat is an aloof and relatively unsociable animal, basically untrainable. Such preconceptions become self-fulfilling prophecies: a kitten will become aloof and distant. Most cats have the potential of being really sociable and friendly.

Many dog owners should have chosen another pet. People who work all day, students who must attend classes, may have to leave the dog at home without companionship or attention. Dogs need companionship; common signs of boredom and loneliness are excessive barking, resistance to housebreaking, and destruction of carpets, drapes, and furniture. Sometimes buying the pet a companion will help, but all too often such dogs are destroyed because they cannot adapt to their owners' life-style.

A more adaptable pet in such situations is the cat. For young professional people, I heartily recommend the cat as the ideal animal companion. Compared to dogs, they are less dependent and get along quite well when left on their own. If you can, get two cats so while you're out they can provide company for each other. They do not have to be housebroken—hard work with a puppy, especially if you live on the tenth floor of a high-rise! Kittens instinctively use a kitty-litter tray. They don't bark, and today, with our crowded buildings and houses, one bark from your dog may bring the police over in no time with a complaint.

In choosing a cat, avoid high-strung breeds like Siamese if you are a novice. Burmese, though expensive, are easygoing, as are Persians, though they tend to be somewhat distant and require much coat care. A good "alley" kitten—the domestic shorthair, the ginger-striped "Heinz," or the tabby/tortoiseshell—is hard to beat. Cats of all varieties vary greatly in temperament, but with careful selection of an outgoing little kitten and the right rearing, most cats will make excellent family pets. Another advantage of cats over dogs is that they require much less attention—for the busy housewife, who so often must care for the pet, this is worth major consideration!

Most dogs need exercise. For an older couple, an invalid, or a city dweller, this need may be difficult to satisfy. In addition, remember that most local authorities have leash laws—one must keep one's dog under restraint at all times. No dog should be allowed to roam free today; but few dogs—and few people for that matter—can tolerate confinement indoors, especially if there is no backyard or garden. And city authorities are now talking about fecal contamination. Would you, as an urban dog owner, be prepared to curb your dog and to pick up its droppings and dispose of them hygienically elsewhere?

I think if you ask yourself *why* you want a pet, we can come close to finding the right one without putting you on the psychoanalyst's couch! Add up your reasons plus your life-style—be you a single person or family member, an apartment dweller or a suburbanite—and it will be relatively easy to find a compatible pet.

I have written two books, *Understanding Your Dog* and *Understanding Your Cat*, which I wish people would read *before* they buy a kitten or puppy. Only too often I receive letters saying if only the owners had known what they know now before they got the pet, they could have avoided some of their problems. Often without the right understanding and rearing the end becomes inevitable—the pet is destroyed. For example, an elderly suburban couple living where there are many free-roaming house dogs were obliged to get rid of their bull terrier. It flew into a rage and tried to attack other unleashed dogs when they walked it on the leash, and was too much for them to handle. Such mismatches are common. But we know enough now about dog and cat behavior and the idiosyncrasies of various breeds to prevent such problems, which cause considerable emotional suffering to pet and owner alike.

Some people feel they need a large watchdog to feel safe. Some go so far as to get an attack-trained dog. *Don't* have your dog attack trained. Trainers often use brutal, inhumane methods, and once your dog is returned to you your family's safety may be jeopardized. The dog may "go off"

Having a pet is, in many ways, like having another child.

and attack without provocation once he has been conditioned to do so. He might attack an innocent stranger coming to your house—a delivery boy, or a neighbor. A child running or playing roughly with one of your own could be attacked. No one can guarantee that an attack-trained dog will attack only on command. Can you always be there to supervise it and always keep it restrained? Burglar alarms are safer, and less costly.

Ownership of attack-trained dogs should be outlawed—since such dogs are more dangerous than any firearm. A gun won't go off by itself. Attack-training schools should be inspected and licensed and ownership restricted to police, security, and military personnel.

Anyone with a large breed of the guard-dog type—German shepherd, Doberman pinscher—should attend obedience school with the dog and become a competent handler. These breeds can be high strung and often are unpredictable. They are naturally protective, and will be even more so if you are shy or nervous. Obedience training is a social necessity.

A good watchdog doesn't need to be big, but it should make plenty of noise. Terriers—fox terriers, Airedales, bull terriers, even little Yorkies—are excellent noise makers. But do remember that your neighbors may object, since a good watchdog will bark at anyone visiting your place—a friend, service person or midnight prowler. Of all the public-nuisance complaints, a dog barking is among the most common.

A single apartment dweller who is absent at work all day or a working couple should not get a dog: get a good burglar alarm system and security locks or find an apartment with top security facilities, and come home to the companionship of one or more cats!

Companionship and protection are two benefits one might desire of a pet. Status is another—a purebred dog or cat with registration papers proving an aristocratic lineage can provide an ego boost.

Remember, though, often there is no better animal than a

"Heinz"—a mongrel cat or dog whose genetic makeup combines the best qualities of both parents—so-called hybrid vigor. Purebreds often suffer from inbreeding and overproduction (with accompanying lack of quality control!) and one is more likely to get a "lemon" in this situation than from the humane shelter adoption center. The advantage of a registered purebred animal is that you have a fair idea beforehand of what it will grow up to look like, and in relation to the breed norm, what kind of temperament it is likely to have. A working beagle, foxhound, or border collie is hardly the right choice for city life. And you know what size a purebred will attain and how much attention its coat will need.

Dogs are more dependent than cats and so are inherently more trainable. I am often asked whether dogs are more intelligent than cats, and which breed of dog is the most intelligent. This kind of thinking just leads us into racist arguments.Intelligence per se is often confused with trainability. A well-socialized dog whose learning is not blocked by fear of overexcitement can be trained more easily than one that is fearful or not well bonded to its owner. The latter will learn less and possibly have a lower I.Q. although it has the same intrinsic intelligence as a more trainable and emotionally stable littermate.

Ideally, if you want a pure-bred animal, spend time, not at a pet store, but at a cat or dog show where you can look at the different breeds and talk to their owners and handlers. This is the best way to learn a good deal about the kind of pet that strikes your fancy. It is easy to be taken in by an appealing, helpless-looking puppy or kitten in a pet store, and a salesperson may pressure you for a decision on the spot. Take a checklist of questions with you (see table). Your selection should be based not upon emotion alone— though emotion certainly does have its place—but on good judgment as well. Remember that buying a kitten or puppy is a responsibility. They are not like houseplants and need more than food, water, and love.

Responsible and irresponsible dog ownership: a free-roaming pack of dogs following a bitch in heat contrasts to the well cared-for, healthy dogs of the show ring.

CHECK LIST

Physical Characteristics: When fully grown, how large will
                 it be?
                 What kind of coat does it have,
                 and will it need much attention?
                 Will it need much exercise? How
                 much living space?
                 Will it require a special diet?
                 Is it subject to any inherited dis-
                 eases (common in some breeds)
                 such as hip dysplasia or blindness?
Once you buy your pet, see your local veterinarian at once.
Discuss with him vaccination, worming, and the pros and
cons of spaying or castrating your pet later.

Emotional Characteristics: Will it be friendly to strangers?
                 Shy or aggressive?
                 How will it be with its own kind—
                 friendly, aggressive?
                 How will it be around children?
                 Will it be easy to train?
                 Learn how to rear and socialize
                 your pet.
                 Will it be generally timid and cau-
                 tious, easygoing, outgoing and
                 bold, active and playful? Poten-
                 tially hyperactive?
                 Will it be independent? Or depend-
                 ent and requiring much attention?
Be sure to instruct your children how to handle and care for
the new pet. If possible, enroll in puppy classes at a local
dog training school.

A newspaper reporter interviewing me about *Understanding Your Cat* confided that, although he had always liked cats and was even more fascinated with them after reading my book, he worried about acquiring one because he might be branded as effeminate or gay. Having been a cat-owning bachelor myself once, I was able to reassure him. Owning and loving a cat is far from effeminate, although I realize some male chauvinists, insecure about their own sexuality, do interpret an interest in cats as "sensitive" and therefore feminine. Having a cat can help establish a rapport with a female guest, provided, of course, she is not allergic to cats or afraid of them. On a first date it is more pleasant to talk about the cat than about the furniture, and a well-socialized cat may make the first move and approach the girl, even lie in her arms!

If you have a family with young children, be sure to instruct them on the needs of a new kitten or puppy, how to handle it and so on. Strict rules must be established right away or trouble may erupt later. My own two children will fight over a little fox or wolf cub that I might bring home to hand-raise. When they were younger, I suspect they might even have pulled the little animal apart if left unsupervised because both wanted to hold it at the same time! Such sibling rivalry must be transmuted into a mutual sharing and caring for the new pet. With children under four or five, you should think twice before getting any pet. Young children are impulsive, unpredictable, and uncoordinated and may frighten or injure a little animal. For a family, I recommend one of the easygoing larger breeds like the golden retriever or Labrador retriever. But if you can stand the pace and have adequate space, a more active dog like a large Airedale or robust Irish terrier, even a standard poodle, can be a great addition to the family. And that is what a new puppy is: an added "child," requiring much work, time, patience, affection, and training if it is to grow up right.

Some people are of the opinion that a cat should not be in a home full of boisterous children. But if a kitten is handled and raised correctly it can be a great source of pleasure to the entire family, high-spirited youngsters included.

Several years ago in London a neighbor called me over to look at his young dog. "It's going daft," he said. From his accent I knew at once he was a Yorkshireman from England's North Country. As a veterinary student I wanted to give the man the impression that I knew my stuff; I began to examine the dog, checking over his eyes, ears, mouth and the other usual parts. "It's now't there young man," he said. "It's in 'is 'ed and tha' conna' see that!"

I was thinking that the dog might have a brain tumor. In fact it was simply hyperactive, becoming quite unmanageable and destructive of everything within reach when left alone in the house. The dog was a young border collie purchased from a farmer. We both realized that it was a working dog that would probably never adapt to suburban life. What he wanted was my stamp of approval to give up the dog, and try to place it on a farm, much as he and his family loved it. Many dogs from working strains—pointers, spaniels, and retrievers—end up, like this border collie, as suburban apartment misfits. Their sad end is often humane destruction.

More recently I had a telephone call from a popular women's magazine concerning a problem about which many of their single women readers had written to them. This is the dog that becomes too possessive of its mistress and is jealous of and aggressive toward male visitors!

Many of these young women obtained dogs primarily for protection. Raised more or less exclusively by its mistress, or perhaps by other females sharing the apartment, such a dog will often become fearful or aggressive toward unfamiliar humans—especially men, and frequently children—because of this restricted socialization. The way around this problem is to insure that, as a puppy, the pet has plenty of contact with a wide variety of people of different ages, of both sexes, and, if possible, of different racial backgrounds. Dogs can be as prejudiced as people if their early socialization is exclusively with one group be it single-white female or urban-black family!

New "mutant" forms of domestic farm animals, such as minihorses, minipigs, and minigoats, can make excellent pets. This minigoat is docile, affectionate, and will never grow large enough to be able to inflict injury.

I have not yet discussed other common pets: goldfish and tropical fish, parrots and parakeets, gerbils and hamsters. They require less attention than cats and dogs, and being preadapted to living in a cage or tank they present fewer problems. It is also less important that your life-style be compatible with their needs, since they are generally less demanding and more self-reliant than cats and dogs. But this isn't always the case, nor are they uninteresting pets. They will be given equal time in later chapters.

Other animals are sometimes kept as pets. Some wild animals, such as opossums, raccoons, foxes, ocelots, and monkeys, have attained a certain popularity as pets. I would hope that you will *not* consider them. The reasons are spelled out in the next chapter. Ownership of undomesticated animals should be restricted to use in research and for some educational purposes, since such animals rarely adapt to captivity and or human life-styles. Many are caught as infants in the world: unnecessary depredation of wild populations not only upsets the balance of nature, but can also lead to extinction of some species. The small jungle cats of South America, for example, prized by the fur industry for their pelts and popular as "exotic" pets, are now threatened with extinction.

Really, there's nothing better than a cat or dog as a pet. No other species has had up to ten thousand years of careful breeding to domesticate it. The end result has been to create reliable pets, able to adapt to the many situations in which our lives and our hearts place them.

Freedom or Restraint— Are You a Responsible Pet Owner?

ARE YOU A responsible pet owner?

Do you let your cat roam freely and go out hunting and courting at night? Is your dog allowed the freedom of the neighborhood, joining other dogs during the day and roaming at will?

To allow pets such freedom may seem natural and humane. The thought of keeping a cat or dog indoors or confined to the yard seems to some cruel and unnatural. Why should our pets endure the privations and restrictions that we ourselves often suffer? We think: at least let our animals live as naturally as possible.

Such sentiments are not compatible with the moral and social ethics of responsible pet ownership. There are ecological and social ramifications of owning a pet today that were almost insignificant just a generation ago. The population of both people and pets has exploded everywhere. It is difficult to gain an overview, the total of the national issues raised by irresponsible pet ownership; your view is limited to your immediate neighborhood and your pet. Consider these figures: there are an estimated 33 million family-owned dogs and 22 million family-owned cats in the United States. Early sexual maturity, short pregnancies, and large litters make cats about forty times more prolific than humans, and dogs fifteen times. Some 415 human beings are born each hour in the United States, and 2,000–3,500 dogs and cats.

Each year some 18 million unwanted animals are handled by humane societies and city animal shelters, at a cost of $25 million. As I said earlier approximately 13 1/2 million unwanted cats and dogs are destroyed each year: this costs an additional $100 million. Nearly 500,000 dogs are put down annually in California alone. Only fourteen of every hundred dogs and nine out of every hundred cats find homes when they wind up at the animal shelter. Sadly enough, to many people pets seem to be nothing more than commodities, simply a source of pleasure, just another possession easily discarded if it is "too much work" or "doesn't work out." Such are the selfish values of a throwaway society.

As a result of exploding populations, the number of reported cases of people being bitten by dogs each year is rising rapidly. Many cases still go unreported. Estimates range from 600,000 to 2 million cases annually, most of the victims children and service personnel. If the dog is not found and held for observation, the victim must undergo a series of extremely painful antirabies injections; some cases require plastic surgery. In 1971, Los Angeles County reported 53,777 dog-bite injuries, St. Louis 2,137, Detroit 8,699, and Baltimore 6,809. Numbers increase with each passing year.

Today, including veterinary services and nonfood pet items, the nation spends $4.5–5.5 billion annually on pets!

Costs associated with rabies control, dog-bite care, sanitation, and public health disease control are at least $50 million a year. One estimate of livestock losses caused by free-roaming dogs stands at $5 million. Total expenditures related to unwanted and free-roaming pets is rising gradually to $200 million a year! A truly staggering figure. Another large figure is the pet-food market: $1.35 billion in 1971 and expected to reach $2 billion this year. Six *billion* pounds of dog and cat food were consumed in 1971.

It has been estimated that the national daily production of dog feces is some 3,500 tons, and dog urine 33 million quarts. Where is all this waste to go?

There are serious diseases that wastes may transmit to people, especially children: leptospirosis is one; another is toxocara, a worm that can migrate in the body and cause blindness and damage to the nervous system. Besides this problem there is the not infrequent inconvenience of footwear and clothing soiled with feces. Trees that are constantly soaked with dog urine may die.

City parks at present rates will soon have to be closed because of the hazards posed by pet wastes. Will there be separate playgrounds for urban dogs, and dog latrines, as exist in London? Will dog owners be fined if they do not pick up their dogs' droppings and dispose of them in sealed plastic bags, or do not keep their dogs always on the leash? Such laws exist already in some places, but enforcement is difficult. The city environment is not the ideal place for some dogs. The attractive alternative, especially for apartment living, is the cat, which uses a litter box indoors and adapts better than most dogs to the confines of an apartment.

If you must let your cat roam free, put a bell on its collar. Although you may think it natural to allow a cat to hunt birds and small animals, the impact of many hunting house cats on the wildlife remaining in suburbia is tremendous. Be kind to the wildlife in your area and bell your cat. If your cat is declawed, never let it out—it cannot defend itself. Perhaps an even greater kindness to any cat is to keep it indoors all the time. It is less likely to be injured in a cat fight, mauled by a free-roaming dog, or struck by an automobile. Kittens can be leash trained, and as adults will enjoy going for short walks with their owners.

It is even more irresponsible to let your dog roam free than it is a cat. Dogs will form packs and can do more damage. Their fecal and urine wastes are more of a health haz-

A common public nuisance is the pack of dogs which gathers around a female in heat. These, and free-roaming house dogs in general, can be a serious public health hazard as well.

ard than those of cats, which often bury their excrement in out-of-the-way places (although sometimes cats will use a sandbox in the park or backyard).

In rural areas, dogs kill farm livestock and compete unfairly with natural predators and scavengers—foxes, coyotes, raccoons, badgers, and skunks, to name a few—for food. But anywhere they roam free house dogs (rather than feral, or wild, dogs that are shy of humans) will bite people; they cause traffic accidents; they fight among themselves, especially over a bitch in heat. Two of the most frequent reasons for seeking veterinary care are pet dogs getting hurt in serious fights or being hit by cars.

Responsible dog ownership therefore entails keeping your dog restrained, at all times. Such responsibility is good not only for your dog, but for other people too.

Many people should not own dogs, but do. Here I am thinking of the couple who both go out to work and must leave the dog unattended all day. A dog is a highly social animal with a deep-seated need for companionship. No wonder such dogs tear up the house, become unhousebroken, hyperactive, overexcited when the owners return, or bark excessively and disturb the neighbors. While muzzling a dog or having its vocal cords removed surgically may stop this nuisance, it will not of course help the underlying emotional problem. Very often all the dog needs is companionship—introducing another dog or a kitten may help, or it may have to be placed in a home where it can be given the attention that it needs.

If pet owners do not assume all the responsibilities of having a pet, then city, state, or federal laws will inevitably be enacted to enforce such responsibility—and soon. Or even more extreme measures may be taken: in Reykjavik, capital of Iceland, no one is allowed to own a dog any more.

I find a life without pets hard to conceive. Many of us would find it unbearable. But in the long run it may be better than having to keep our pets always confined and under control. Some pets adapt better than others, some breeds of dog being easier to manage than others. Of the enormous numbers of unwanted cats and dogs destroyed each year some do reflect a lack of concern or understanding on the part of their former owners. Some of these animals undoubtedly are unable to adapt for one reason or another to the human environment.

In the near future there will be greater selection in favor of pet breeds having the temperament to adapt to the conditions our life-styles impose. In fact, such selection is going on right now. Many breeds of dog once used for performing specific kinds of work seem to be genetically adapting over here to a new role as household companions. We can help our pets adapt even better by having them neutered. Castration and spaying will make life much easier, removing natural frustrations. A neutered pet is often easier to handle, less aggressive, less likely to pine, scream, scratch, whine, or even bite to be let out.

Responsible ownership involves more than obeying the laws and local ordinances. It also involves understanding the behavior and the emotional needs of the pet and developing the ability to communicate with and control it. Some of the social and ecological consequences of irresponsible pet ownership have been outlined. It is a serious problem of increasing magnitude today. If you are not a 100 per cent responsible pet owner, I hope that you will begin to be one tomorrow.

Love alone is not enough for your pet; neither is providing the best diet and veterinary care. Understanding is essential. The owner must understand the needs, emotions and behavior of the pet *distinct from his or her own projections and expectations*, for the physical and mental well-being of man and animal both.

Homeless feral and free-roaming domestic dogs of the city do not fare well in such a hostile environment. Irresponsible ownership leads to road accidents, disease, starvation, and death. Rarely do they survive for long, an exception being this pack of three dogs from St. Louis.

3

Love Is Not Enough

I'M SURE YOU love your pet, but there are some areas of pet ownership where even the most well-intentioned owners fall short. As you read, rate yourself as to what kind of pet owner you are.

Understanding

Do you make a real attempt to understand—by reading and observation and conversation with other pet owners—the true nature and personality of the animal you live with? For instance, it is important to know that there are critical times early in the life of a pet when lasting emotional attachments and impressions are made. Even the kindest owners may frustrate a young puppy or kitten by misinterpreting developmental behavior. A kitten, for instance, is not merely being naughty but is exploring the world around it—with perhaps unwanted enthusiasm.

Some parents make the mistake of treating a little girl like A Little Girl, not as a child with its own needs and wants. She is handled gently, and rough-and-rumble activities that

35

she might enjoy are reserved for little boys. Similarly, people will engage in rough-and-tumble with a puppy, but few will roughhouse with their cat even though many kittens love such play. Our own personal expectations lead us to stereotype our children into roles that may please us but not be right for *them*—and I believe a similar process goes on with pets.

Compatibility

Why do you have a pet? Is it for companionship? For the security of having a guard dog? For status, or as a subject of conversation in your home? Or is it simply another toy for the children? With all this in mind, think about whether your pet is compatible with your needs and your life-style.

Is yours a busy house filled with children or hectic activities? If so, does your pet really get sufficient time and attention? Does your pet have a space to call its own and the privacy it might need in such an active household? After it matures, who will give the animal its training (a consideration that's especially important for a dog)? Only too often, when a puppy grows up, the children lose interest in it, and it becomes the mother's job. And then the pet may become a chore instead of a delight for the whole family.

Care

How well do you care for your pet? Do you feed it whenever it announces it's hungry? That's the kind of love that kills. Do you feed it the best of meat and fish? This, too, will kill. Dogs and cats, especially those confined indoors, need a very carefully regulated diet. A number of today's commercially available foods are scientifically formulated and balanced diets that will insure good health and a long life. But too many pets today are overindulged and overfed,

Love is not enough.   *(Glenn McClurg, HSUS)*

and would live longer and healthier lives if owners were more knowledgeable about their nutrition and care.

How often do you take your pet to the veterinarian for a routine health check? When did your dog or cat have its last booster shot of vaccine for infectious viral disease? Does your dog have its rabies tag? Your cat or dog should also have vaccinations against those diseases that it can get from its own kind—canine or feline distemper, canine hepatitis and leptospirosis, and feline pneumonitis. There are also some diseases that your pet can give you and your children. Do you obey the rule of washing your hands before meals, especially after playing with your pet?

Respect

Do you really respect your pet? Is your relationship one where you appreciate and value the pet for *itself*—not as an extension of your own emotions and projections, but as an independent creature with its own needs, strengths, and fallibilities?

Perhaps, of course, the pet exploits *you*, in which case you might have an overdependent or delinquent pet on your hands. If your pet uses manipulative tactics, such as whining and sulking, to get its own way, you must evaluate yourself as to how consistent you are in giving your pet attention and discipline. Fluctuations in your mood and behavior can only confuse a pet and make it feel insecure in your presence.

Ultimately, out of respect for your pet comes a reverence for all life—a moral and ethical understanding which adds greatly to relationships between human and human as well as between human and animal.

Pet-owner Evaluation Form

Here are a few questions for you to check over to see if

you as a pet owner—or prospective pet owner—are doing the right thing for your pet. If you can't answer all the questions satisfactorily, then read on and find the right answers, or a more suitable pet to fit your life-style.

Your Life-style

1. Is there usually someone at home during the day to take care of the pet?
2. Are you away from home for extended periods?
3. Do you think you would take your dog out twice a day for long walks?
4. Do you have the time, know-how, and patience to housebreak and train a dog?
5. If you have expensive furniture, are you prepared to train your cat not to claw, or to have it declawed?
6. Is the breed you choose compatible with *your* temperament and physical health? If in doubt, check it out.
7. Are there local ordinances or housing regulations that would impose restrictions on you and your pet?
8. If you intend to keep your dog outdoors, do you have a secure yard or adequate cage and a good kennel?
9. Are you prepared for the essential expenses of veterinary treatment and preventive vaccinations? If your dog is a large breed, can you afford to feed it the quantity of food that it needs? Are you also prepared to have your pet neutered? And are you familiar with the reasons?
10. Have you read any good books on understanding your pet, on feeding in general, and on training? Do this before you get a pet, and if it is a purebred, read up on the breed first: forewarned is forearmed!

Others in the Family

1. Are you or is anyone in your family allergic to cats or dogs?

2. Is the wife expected to take charge of all feeding, cleaning, and training?

3. If there is an animal already in your home, can you be sure it will accept a new pet? When did this animal last have a physical checkup? Does it need "booster" shots, and does it wear an identification tag on its collar in case it gets lost? Do you know how to introduce them correctly right away?

4. If there is a child in the home, is that child old and responsible enough to treat the pet with kindness and understanding and to care for it effectively if it is the child's designated responsibility? If there is more than one child, is one at least able to do both?

5. If a human baby is expected, if it is Christmastime, or if you are soon to be moving house—can you wait a while before you get a new pet?

4

How to Choose and Use
Your Veterinarian

AN AUNT OF mine in England had two Pekingese dogs.
They were her "children" and enjoyed every indulgence.
She gave them what she thought was the best of everything—slivers of roast beef, lambs' kidneys, padded har-
nesses so their leashes wouldn't rub against their skins and
buckle-on coats to wear when it was cold or wet outdoors.
They were attended by the vet with the best reputation in
the country, and they had regular checkups every six
months. My aunt never went anywhere, even on vacation,
if she couldn't take them with her. Then one day she had to
be hospitalized for surgery and a prolonged recovery. Fear-
ing that her two dogs would pine away if she put them in a
kennel, she made what she thought was the kindest decision. She had them both put to sleep!

This is an extreme example of killing with kindness.
More common is the pet that is indulged with the wrong diet
and dies from obesity and kidney failure or has a mouth full
of rotting teeth. Or the pet whose owner panders it its every
whim, producing an overdependent, delinquent monster or
a hypochondriac with psychosomatic aches and pains. Of
course we all want the best for our pets, but we must always

41

be on the watch to prevent an "overkill" of solicitude.

If we really do want the best for them, the most realistic first step is to get the best veterinarian possible. With his guidance and a few sensible rules of thumb, you can reasonably assure your pet's health without being exploited by others in the pet business who play on your emotional bond with your animal.

As a student. I trained with several different veterinarians, and they were all sound and honest professionals. They knew their job and, if they had a difficult case, they would not hesitate to seek a second opinion from colleagues in the district. Some vets (and doctors for humans, too) consider it an admission of failure to seek a second opinion. Fortunately, such immaturity is rare today, and competition among different practitioners (some were even reduced to stealing clients) is being replaced by cooperation. This is largely a result of the formation of local, regional, and national veterinary associations. These professional groups are valuable to you as a pet owner. They don't do any price fixing, but they do try to maintain fair fees. More important, like the American Animal Hospital Association, they set up reasonable standards of medical and surgical practice and facilities.

What are the qualifications of a good veterinarian? First of all, he or she must be thoroughly trained at a state-approved veterinary college, and must pass a state examination in order to practice. Other than that, a doctor's reputation and your own good sense must guide you. For instance, older vets may seem "rustier" than more recent graduates, but they have a wealth of experience that no amount of expensive equipment and waiting-room facilities can outweigh.

When choosing a vet, remember that it's not always advisable to go by another pet owner's opinion. They can only judge subjectively. A vet can be branded rotten simply because he has a brisk, impersonal manner. Another may simply be too busy to squander his time with an oversensitive owner. A doctor may be disliked because he gave the owner a large bill and never cured Fido of his problem. Yet some diseases are incurable. Yes, do ask the opinions of other pet owners—but consider their own personalities as you evaluate their replies.

Vets themselves are generally reluctant to be frank about colleagues who may not be the best specialists. Feelings of professional etiquette often keep them from speaking with candor. One way around this is to call a local pet store, humane society, or animal shelter for a recommendation. If there is a state veterinary school nearby, you have it made; the best facilities, an array of specialists and eager students to examine your animal are at your disposal. And don't be put off by the fact that student work is involved. If a trainee treats your pet you can be assured it is under strict professional supervision!

Once you have settled on a vet, learn to use him correctly. Routine checkups should be on a regular schedule— twice a year, in the spring and fall. Take a stool sample to be examined for parasites every six months. Have your dog tested for heart worms in the spring. Cats and dogs should have an annual rabies vaccination or an annual booster for other viral infections. A visit once a year is thus the minimum and should be obligatory.

Most vets do not make house calls since it would be too costly and time-consuming. Even in emergencies, it's best to take the pet to the hospital rather than insisting on a house call since all the emergency equipment (oxygen tent, surgical materials, whole blood for transfusions, and so on) is at the hospital. Mobile hospital units are generally impractical.

Ask your vet for advice on diet, grooming, general care, inoculation schedules, and neutering, as well as guidelines for recognizing certain diseases. Most hospitals or clinics have a variety of brochures on these subjects for you to take home and read.

Don't be afraid to ask the veterinarian questions; when in doubt, phone him. Simply give the doctor a straightforward explanation of what the symptoms are. And don't feel he is being curt when he makes you stick to a descriptive and unemotional account of your pet's problem.

Only too often an owner will wait out the first signs of illness, becoming more and more worried as the night progresses, finally calling the poor vet in the early hours of the morning. When in doubt, waste no time; a pet that is allowed to get sicker and sicker may be beyond the combined curative powers of both your vet and Mother Nature. A diagnosis cannot always be made on the telephone, but that is the place to start.

Bills for veterinary services can be a shock, especially if the bill for surgery and medication is $250—and the animal itself was given to you free. Remember, many of the drugs and surgical procedures used are identical to the ones used on humans, and vets have at least as much training as the average medical doctor. If you want good veterinary treatment for your pet, you must be prepared to pay for it.

Some companies compete with legitimate treatment by offering pet owners nonprescription medicines that can be bought over the counter in pet stores. Worm medicines, "health powders," coat conditioners, and the like are generally a waste of time and money. If your pet is out of condition, don't go to the pet store; see your veterinarian. In the long run, this will be less costly for you and much better for your pet.

I have seen some of the consequences of home-doctoring "treatments"—pouring gasoline on a skin infection or giving a sick puppy fresh garlic. Generally, the illness is prolonged until it's too late for the vet to insure a cure.

If you're planning to go on vacation without your pet, your vet may also be able to advise you about boarding facilities. The local humane society or animal shelter may also know of a good boarding place—call them, as well as pet-owning neighbors—or you may simply have to find a kennel in the Yellow Pages. In any case, here are a few guidelines for judging a boarding place:

Visit the kennel and notice how the staff relates to the

animals in their pens. Do they talk to them or ignore them? Do they take the time to exercise the dogs? Are the animal runs clean? Do they cater to individual food preferences? (Some dogs may not take to institutional fare.)

A good boarding kennel should inform you of special health measures you should take prior to your pet's arrival, such as vaccinations.

They should also give you some guarantee of your pet's being kept in good health—will the kennel foot the veterinary bills should your animal incur any accident during his stay?

Dogs generally adapt better than cats to boarding, although dependent ones may suffer adversely from sudden and prolonged separation from home and owner. If your dog is very attached to you, drop it off for a couple of days at the boarding kennel several weeks before your actual departure, then bring it home again. This way your pet will realize that it's not going to be in the kennel forever and that you will be back again to collect it.

For a cat, try to get a house sitter to come in once a day to care for it. Cats can be very disturbed by a change in their environment, and keeping them at home is a better alternative to a sojourn in a boarding kennel. There are, however, some excellent boarding "catteries," which your vet should be able to tell you about. Your cat may need booster vaccines a couple of weeks before being boarded to protect it from some diseases.

A final note on some relevant pet products.

Carrier Cages or Boxes

They must be chewproof and crushproof; they should have enough room in them for your pet to be able to turn around and sit up; ventilation holes must be on all four sides of the box, and on the top, just in case the carrier is ever wedged in on three sides. I don't like the open-wire

crates because they do not give the animal sufficient security and protection from the elements. Three opaque, ven-
tilated sides and a front grill for the pet to peek out is ideal.

Leashes and Collars

All qualities are available, but I would buy good quality
material simply because it lasts longer. A cat collar (carry-
ing identification tag and a bell to warn birds if you must let
your cat roam free) should contain a piece of elastic material. If the cat accidentally gets caught by its collar on a fence
or tree branch, it should be able to slip it off without too
much difficulty. If you are unable to find a collar like this in
a local store, just cut your cat's collar apart and sew in a
piece of elastic yourself.

5

Pet Foods and Pet Feeding

ONLY A FEW years ago most people fed their dogs table scraps mixed with dog biscuits or dry meal. Some would even boil up good butcher's scraps with a few vegetables for their cats and dogs.

Today, with smaller families and fewer table scraps and the widespread replacement of the local butcher by meat-packing plants supplying chain stores, feeding a pet a varied and nutritious diet can be a problem. This responsibility has largely been assigned to the manufacturers of pet foods. As with any consumer-oriented company, it is often difficult to evaluate their advertising propaganda: their claims are designed to sell their product and the adequacy of their product as a complete balanced diet for the pet is often a question they avoid. Some companies are blatantly unethical, guilty of misinforming the public, such as stating that your pet needs an all-meat diet. An all-meat diet can be stressful to an older pet with liver or kidney problems, and may cripple a growing kitten or puppy. A diet consisting solely of red tuna fish can cause yellow fat disease in cats.

Both cats and dogs are carnivores. In the wild, meat eaters balance their diet naturally by ingesting carbohydrates in the form of vegetable material from the digestive systems of their prey. They also eat certain internal organs rich in vitamins before they eat the "meat," which is muscle that contains little more than protein and iron.

What, then, is a balanced diet for a cat or dog? Palatability is a critical factor—the odor, taste, and consistency of the various products influence your pet's preferences. Fortunately food types range widely from the moist (canned), to the semimoist (in plastic packs), to the dry meal or biscuit type. The latter may be the best for your pet, keeping gums and teeth healthy; a constant diet of moist food can lead to dental problems.

Unfortunately, many pampered pets do not find the dry foods very palatable. Adding a little water, beef stock, or table scraps can make it more acceptable, but add a quantity larger than one-fourth of the whole diet; otherwise the nutritional balance may be upset. Dry foods—which are scientifically balanced and safe—are more economical to feed. A can of moist food is 75 percent water! It is a myth that dry foods contain a high ash content that can cause calculi or stones to form in the urinary tract: diet alone is not the cause. Dry foods are not entirely cereal. They usually contain some dried animal protein and fat and in addition, vegetable protein from soybean, which is highly nutritious for animal and man both. Dry foods for cats should contain 8 percent fat, 8 to 10 percent moisture, and 30 percent protein. For adult dogs, the protein content may be lower; it should remain around 30 percent for puppies and toy breeds. Since the dry food doesn't spoil, it can be fed ad lib—a ration being given for the pet to nibble on as it pleases, provided the pet doesn't overeat.

Remember, most of the better-known pet foods today are scientifically well formulated and balanced, taking into account the various problems that I have mentioned. The pet owner can make things worse, disturbing such balanced diets by giving too much table scraps or hamburger, or adding excessive amounts of vitamins such as A and D. A balanced food provides two basic things—calories for energy and nutritional (body-building) elements. Vitamins, minerals (ash), essential fatty acids, protein, fat, and carbohydrate are all added in the right proportions. Adding extras yourself could upset this balance. With too much raw meat, for example, your pet will not get enough minerals, vitamins, and carbohydrates. Too much fat will satisfy its calorie requirements—but it will have difficulty eating enough to obtain the essential nutritional elements.

Read the label on the dog-food can and check the proportions against table 1. Cereal grains provide the necessary carbohydrates and bulk fiber; if yeast, corn, soybean, or wheat has been added, your pet will have the necessary B vitamins and essential fatty acids. Bone meal provides the right proportions of calcium and phosphorus and iodized salt, sodium, iodine, and chlorine balance. If the proteins are mainly of animal origin, and also of good quality, then your pet will have the necessary assimilable proteins.

Table 1

Basic Nutrient Requirements (wet weight percentages)

	Water	Protein*	Fat	Carbo-hydrate	Ash	Calcium	Total solids
Adult Cats	70%	14%	10%	5%	1.0%	0.6%	30%
Adult Dogs	75%	6%	1.4%	17%	0.3%	0.3%	25%

*Protein must be of high quality (meat, liver). Low-quality protein containing much connective tissue (lungs) is poorly utilized. Overcooked foods may contain denatured proteins which will not be absorbed.

A cat needs a different diet (see table). It is important to avoid feeding your cat an all-meat (beef or fish) product; this should be the evening treat. Their basic diet should consist of a balanced semimoist or dry food fed ad lib.

It is necessary to read the list of ingredients and note their proportions in the composition of the many varieties of canned foods available today. Some luxury canned foods are suitable only for an occasional treat, since some of them contain 95 percent meat, with minerals and vitamins added. Others containing less protein and having more cereal as "bulk" may be used as an everyday food. Still, canned foods contain a lot of moisture, and I for one don't like paying for water! Some of the semimoist packaged foods, those which contain at least 20 per cent protein and up to 35 per cent moisture, may be used as a daily feed.

Remember that the drier the food, the more water your pet will need. Caution should be exercised when feeding semi-moist and dry foods, especially to larger dogs: after a big meal, and especially after a hot day, the dog may drink excessively, and this may result in acute bloat or gastric torsion. While milk is a useful supplement for weaning pups and kittens and for lactating mothers, it is no substitute for water. Being high in lactose sugar, it may cause diarrhea in both cats and dogs. Make sure that your pet doesn't have drinking water that has been filtered through a water softener. It may then be deprived of certain essential minerals and trace elements not found in its food which some believe may contribute to urinary calculus formation.

If your pet is greedy, divide its daily ration into smaller portions fed at intervals. Canned food from the refrigerator served still chilled may be less palatable to your pet, and if eaten quickly may be rejected by the stomach. Let it warm slightly but don't let it spoil. With good, balanced pet diets readily available today, nutritional disorders are not as common as they once were. Often, a pet may develop a taste for an unbalanced diet, thus creating additional stress with disease, increased possibility of internal parasites, and additional problems with pregnancy, lactation, and aging.

Spaying or castration may lower the general activity of the pet, making it more likely to put on weight. Boredom, too, is a factor: an animal (or person) with little else to do may eat more than is needed. When the pet dictates to the owner what it will and will not eat, the problem is one of relationship. The owner's will *must* prevail; although the pet may go on a starvation protest for a while. A hungry animal *will* eventually eat, although some stubborn ones may need a veterinarian's help: an injection of B vitamins to stimulate the appetite and break their refractoriness.

Few people realize that their house cat is descended from a living desert animal; its ancestor is *Felis lybica*, the Kaffir or desert cat. This is why cats drink so little water compared to the dog. Like most desert-adapted animals, it conserves water by concentrating its urine. In the wild, it rarely needs to drink; its prey is 70 per cent water and water can be derived from ingested fat besides. Unlike dogs, cats normally obtain about 60 per cent of their calories from fat. Wild cats depend totally upon the livers of their prey as their source of vitamin A; all cat foods have (or should have) this vitamin added if there is no liver contained in the preparation. Cats and dogs do not normally need vitamin C, which they are able to manufacture in their livers. During disease or under the stress of pregnancy, however, vitamin C supplementation is sometimes necessary.

Thiaminase, an enzyme which destroys thiamin (one of the B vitamins), is present in some fish; most companies add this vitamin to allow for possible loss in the preparation of foods. Fish foods, and especially red tuna fish, may also be high in fats; in the absence of vitamin E or an artificially added antioxidant, they can cause yellow fat disease or steatorrhea in cats. Absence of this vitamin in dogs may cause muscular dystrophy, decrease exercise tolerance, and possibly affect the muscles of the heart. Rancid (oxidized) fat also destroys vitamin A.

Feed your pet *at regular times*. In the wild, animals hunt at a particular time of day; their lives are quite regimented. Regular feeding will help insure a steady appetite and regularity in elimination. I personally like a self-feeding system where the cat or dog may help itself any time to a hopper or dish of dry or semimoist food during the day. Then for the evening meal they are given a canned "treat" or a few table scraps. Provided the pet doesn't overeat (and that is rare) they thrive if given the opportunity to regulate their own food intake by the self-feeding or ad lib method. It gives the pet something to do during the day and helps break up the monotony. Dogs may become less destructive in the home and in kennels, less prone to coprophagy (eating feces).

It may seem unkind to feed your pet the same brand of food every day. This is anthropomorphic thinking. We are omnivores and so naturally enjoy variety; dogs and cats are carnivores and in the wild would have a relatively monotonous diet too. A little variety is not undesirable, but switching brands erratically (say as the result of a sale at the store) can cause severe digestive upset. If you raise your pet right, it won't give you problems later as a finicky eater. If you must change over to a different diet, always do it gradually. It is less of a shock to the system and more acceptable generally to the pet if you add slowly increasing amounts of the new food to its old menu.

On a well-balanced diet, your pet should not have diarrhea. If it has, it may have a bowel infection, such as coccidiosis, and you should consult your veterinarian. If it is constipated, too much rich food low in fiber bulk is usually to blame. Balanced commercial foods include small amounts of fiber to prevent this problem.

Cats are all roughly the same size. But dogs range in size from Great Dane to Chihuahua and it is important to remember that *the larger the dog, the fewer calories per pound of body weight are required.* Also, temperament influences how much food they need—a more active dog requires more food than a less active littermate. In the case of young, fast-growing pets and/or lactating mothers, much food is needed; to avoid bloating and indigestion, the daily ration should be divided into three or more feedings.

When pregnant, your pet needs 20 percent more food. If she is on a self-feeding system, she will make her own adjustments. She will also adjust for the 2½–3 times more food per day that she will need when she is nursing her offspring. For the growing, weaned animal, doubling the usual adult maintenance level of food is the rule; again, if weaned onto a self-feeding (i.e. self-regulating) system, pups and kittens will thrive. They won't gorge themselves through eating competitively each time you feed them. For very fast-growing pups—Great Danes, wolfhounds—*don't* give large amounts of vitamin A and D to aid in skeletal growth: excess is as bad as none. A little steam-sterilized bone meal is the ideal mineral supplement when a little lightly cooked liver is added. All kittens and pups should be checked for worms and other diseases as infestation or infection will affect the assimilation of food for development and so their growth.

Working dogs need to be provided with more energy in the form of fat and carbohydrate than simply feeding them more meat; protein is an inefficient source of energy. A working dog may need additional supplementation of vitamin E and two of the B vitamins, thiamin and riboflavin. A light meal a couple of hours before working is recommended.

The older pet needs high-quality protein because, with the impaired kidney function that results from age, much protein is lost in the urine. Trying to remedy this by supplying too much protein, however, may stress the liver and kidneys and cause severe uremia, possibly death. The older pet is less active and needs less fat and carbohydrate. Supplementation of the following is indicated for the older pet: vitamins A, B complex, D, and E, iron, and bone meal (for calcium and phosphorus).

Too much fat in the older pet may lead to an even greater loss of calcium, and the resultant osteoporosis is a common problem in aging animals and man alike. The B vitamins are needed to facilitate carbohydrate breakdown; the latter, derived from cereals, should be well cooked to break down the starch granules so they may be more easily assimilated. For an old dog, a homemade ration may benefit the pet considerably. It should consist of: boiled rice, farina, or oatmeal; cottage cheese or boiled eggs; ground lean meat and organs; liver pancreas or kidneys; with vitamin and mineral supplements added. Add a little table salt to encourage the dog to drink and keep its kidneys functioning well. (But an old dog with heart trouble, like a human, must be kept on a special low-salt diet.)

For an overweight dog that must go on a diet, avoid cereals and fatty foods; instead, give it lean ground meat, liver, kidneys, cottage cheese, and boiled eggs, mixed with almost equal proportions of a green leafy vegetable or rice (for bulk), supplemented with minerals and vitamins. Feed the pet twice daily. A thirty-pound dog should diet on about one pound of this mixture daily. You will have to experiment a little to find just the right amount for your pet.

Dogs and teething puppies enjoy chewing—beef thigh bones or knuckle bones or dry rawhide. Softer bones may splinter and cause internal injury or severe obstruction. Cats and dogs like to eat fresh grass. It may be a tonic, or it may be a way of adding bulk to help clean out the alimentary tract.

Pets are not people, and they will not thrive on people food. Too many people kill their pets with love: overindulgence with unbalanced foods will shorten their lives considerably. I hope that this review has helped you understand the nutritional needs of your pet and will help you improve the well-being of your animal companions. Love alone is not enough.

6

Sex and the Single Pet

IN MY MAIL I receive frequent enquiries about the sexual needs of pet cats and dogs (but no letters of solicitation, although a man did once try to arrange a date for his shepherd with my she-wolf!). Some owners are rightfully concerned about the sex lives of their pets which, for a housebound dog or cat, may be nothing short of owner-enforced celibacy. Is this cruel or inhumane? How about some of the sexual problems that arise in a frustrated, fully sexed pet? In this chapter I will tackle some of these problems, hoping to make life easier for some pets and at the same time to ease the consciences of concerned owners.

A consideration of sex and the single pet would lack perspective without taking into consideration the intriguing sex lives of wild animals (and of the human animal as well).

Wild carnivores—mountain lions, bobcats, coyotes, and wolves—have a short breeding season once every year. In contrast, their domesticated cousins, cats and dogs, have two (and sometimes more) breeding seasons in a year; the males, instead of having seasonal heats like the females, are *always* in heat. One might wonder, what this does to the psyche of pets. Domestication, where selective breeding is used to keep fertile animals with desired characteristics "productive," has had a profound effect on their sexual cycles, and seems to have had a greater effect on the males than on the females. It is a phenomenal leap for a male animal, at one time a seasonal breeder, to be perpetually in heat once he is mature. Perhaps man has created his pets in his own image; man stands out among the animal kingdom as the one species where both male and female are (at least in theory!) constantly receptive.

Sex fulfills several important nonreproductive functions in man: relieving emotional and physical tensions, providing a source of sensual pleasure, and, perhaps, even transcendental "oceanic" experiences. Socially speaking, its most important function may be to maintain the pair bond and so preserve the integrity and stability of the family nucleus. If his mate were only periodically receptive, the human male would seek other mates, thus disrupting the original pair bond unless he, too, became (like a male wolf) sexually active in synchrony with his mate. In the former state he would resemble our domesticated male cats and dogs, whose continual sexual appetite is continuously being frustrated by the absence of females in a state of sexual receptivity! Most cats and dogs do show spring and fall peaks of sexual activity (and seasonal influences on human sexual activity are recognized). But not all female cats and dogs follow the spring and fall cycle: some have a summer and winter pattern.

Social Aspects

One reviewer, in commenting on *Understanding Your Cat*, was moved to challenge my statement that women living together tend to have synchronized menstrual cycles. This *has* been sceintifically validated and it brings to light an important phenomenon: namely that social stimuli may have a profound effect on a number of sexual functions, including the timing of ovulation, sexual receptivity, conception, and fertility of the male.

A ring dove, hearing the coos of a male or seeing him make his courtship display, shows rapid development of her ovaries and oviducts when compared to an isolated female. A stud bull, whose semen is collected artifically for insemination and who has been deprived of the company of cows and playful heifers, may produce less sperm. His fertility will increase once he is allowed into the company of even sexually nonreceptive cows. Large colonies of animals, such as cliff-nesting gulls and "rookeries" of penguins and seals, tend to produce their young in synchrony—and more young are produced, proportionately, than in smaller colonies. Here, social stimulation—the rivalry fights and displays of males to determine "pecking order" and the courtship ceremonies of pairing animals—has a potentiating effect on the hormonal systems of others in the group.

Kennel owners have told me of an impressive synchrony of estrus (heat) in some dogs. They believe there may be an element of competition between dogs (but this is debatable). What happens is that an older bitch with a well-established cycle may come into heat earlier if a younger bitch near her is in heat. This probably is more related to social synchrony than competitiveness.

Such social stimulation is not vital for man or dog. But it may play an important part in the reproductive success of cats. The caterwauling of courting toms probably has a stimulating effect on the queens, as well as stimulating (and provoking) the competing males. The penis of the tomcat has small barbs which cause intense stimulation in the female and make her ovulate reflexively. The reflex response may be sensitized by caterwauling before mating.

Bitches do not ovulate when stimulated; like the human female they have a cycle more directly under the control of internal processes. We cannot rule out the importance of external factors, though. The "tie"—when two mating dogs remain locked together for 15 or 20 minutes—may have a potentiating effect upon fertility; in man, intense excitement of fear and rage (as in the case of rape) may increase the probability of a fertile union.

Sex and Love

The long receptive period of human females has a social, as well as a reproductive purpose; only a few animals have a longer one. (Baboons and lions are two examples.) What is it, then, that keeps together a pair of coyotes that only have sex during a couple of weeks in the year, or swans, which also pair up for life? A purely affectional bond, independent of sex—love, if you wish—must be involved. It is of course also involved in the pairing of humans, hence the confusion that often exists between love and sexuality.

Sexual attachments in any animal (including man) are the source of much jealousy and conflict. Take, for example, the daily problem I face when I take our male and female dogs out for a walk in the park. The female, Tiny, is much more aggressive toward female dogs when I take her for a walk than when my wife does. And this makes life difficult for Benji, her male companion, who wants to play with most of the females he meets! Further complications arise when we meet male dogs—especially big ones. Tiny makes goo-goo eyes and solicits play; Benji, trembling with possessiveness and jealousy, has to be restrained firmly with the leash or he will attack—even if the other dog is four times his size!

Sex and Odors (Pheromones)

More than one owner has written to me about the effect of a new perfume or after-shave lotion on his dog. Some perfumes contain ingredients that make some dogs become quite amorously aroused. The animal is naturally confused by such an ambiguous signal from its owner!

Courtship between she-wolf and malamute dog (bowing) involves elaborate rituals and communication, including bowing, dancing, hugging embraces, and finally mounting.

Cats, too, are very sensitive to certain odors. A cat "turned on" by a smell will open its mouth slightly, blink a little, and look somewhat "stoned." This is called the *Flehmen response* and is probably the result of stimulation of a second smell system associated with sexuality (see *Understanding Your Cat* for more details).

A cat coming home after a night out with the boys may be attacked by a resident companion cat. This isn't a form of punishment for "catvorting"; it simply is a not uncommon response to a change in odor. The smell of strange cats if it persists on another cat may trigger its companion to attack.

Even general excitement can trigger sexual actions in cats and dogs. This is quite normal. A dog aroused during play may suddenly attempt to mount its human or canine playmate. My own neutered tomcat always tries to mount his companion cat, a spayed female, whenever they go for a ride in the car!

Intense arousal in human females—a deflowered virgin or a rape victim—also increases the chances of fertilization; this is a rather disturbing aspect of the emotional influences on ovulation.

Excitement can work the other way, though—emotional stress, as when a bitch is shipped to a kennel for breeding, can switch off the heat. Then when the unbred dog returns home, she comes back into heat again. So much for arranged marriages!

Courtship

The courtship activities of wild animals, of a wolf, a bull moose, or a peacock, are beautiful to behold. In contrast, a stud dog, stallion, or bull simply mounts the female, which is often forcibly restrained. The exquisite ritual of courtship is eliminated or subdued by man in the mating of many of his domesticated animals.

Psychiatrists and counselors recognize that man often behaves like the animals he has domesticated: "courtship" (caressing, foreplay) is often absent. The female, unsatisfied, may experience frigidity and the marriage bond may be endangered. Therapy involves reestablishing a "courtship" phase prior to the consummatory act. But how many busy people, I wonder, have the time, patience, or energy for lovemaking? Man is not a nocturnal animal, but out of habit and convenience sex is often confined to nighttime at the end of a hard day's work.

Abnormal Attachments

Experiments with animals have shown that some species, if raised exclusively with people, become so imprinted upon humans that when they reach sexual maturity they will refuse to mate with their own kind. Instead, they show obvious sexual preference toward their human foster parents. I have known many dogs and cats, of both sexes, that are so closely attached to their owners that they will never mate with their own kind. What a tragic confusion! What a lifetime of unrequited love and sexuality! (Occasionally this is encouraged: since the beginning of man's relationship with animals, some men and women have engaged in bestiality.) It would certainly be a kindness to such imprinted pets to neuter them before they reach sexual maturity.

I believe it is a kindness to our pets to have them neutered *before* they are fully mature and before they have had sexual experience. This way they won't feel deprived and they will certainly never be frustrated. It is a pathetic sight to see a cat in heat rolling and calling night after night or a bitch whining and tearing at the door to get out, especially when the owners have no intentions of breeding them. More psychological damage is done by *not* spaying than by spaying. In fact, a spayed cat or dog is often a more tractable pet, and a castrated cat usually won't spray in the house and give carpets and drapes his personal identity. Altered pets won't contribute to the present overpopulation of unwanted pets by being accidentally mated. But owning a spayed pet is no excuse for letting it roam outside freely just because it can't get pregnant.

For some reason, people are more reluctant to have their tomcat or male dog castrated. Is it because since it is the human female who usually takes steps to safeguard herself against pregnancy it is all right to do the same to a female dog or cat? Or is it because the human male vicariously identifies with the sexuality of an entire male pet? To castrate it may be a threat to his own virility!

As we have modified our own sexuality in order to adapt to modern life, so we must help our pets adapt better, too. In domesticating them we have made them sexually precocious—they mature faster than their wild cousins—and sexually promiscuous, and have given them a much stronger sex drive, now not limited to one short breeding season annually. In earlier times this was of much value—more cats and dogs could be bred in a given time, a real asset in artificially evolving and propagating new strains and breeds. But today, with an overabundance of cats and dogs, such attributes are no longer of primary importance (and perhaps are not even desirable). We must consider the psychological well-being of our pets, their "mental health." One way, as is currently practiced in Denmark, would be to provide our pets with special kennel facilities where they could satisfy their sexual desires with resident animals in an artificially induced state of sexual receptivity for the "clients."

A more convenient alternative is to neuter. It is part of man's responsibility as a pet owner. Some take the position that we are not considering the animal's rights, since it has no say in the matter. But if I were a young kitten or puppy, I would ask you to take me to the spay clinic tomorrow. Better to be ignorant and at peace than confused and frustrated!

7

Your Pet's World of Smell

DO YOU KNOW why your dog insists on rolling in the most obnoxious-smelling things? Why your cat likes to back up against the furniture and drapes and fill the entire house with his odor? Understanding may not make such behavior more acceptable to you. But at least understanding can help you enter a world mostly foreign to us: the world of smell. Unlike cats and dogs, we have a poorly developed sense of smell. We rely less on our noses than on our eyes and ears. So-called primitive people, like the bushmen of Australia, have an extremely well-developed sense of smell: probably our cultural upbringing has done much to dampen this sense.

Dogs and cats have a singular advantage over us in that they possess a second organ of smell, known as Jacobson's organ or the vomeronasal organ. It is situated in the nasal cavity just above and behind the upper front teeth. Two small ducts behind the incisor teeth pass through the hard palate from the mouth cavity into the organ. Odors that enter the mouth may be sniffed and tongued into these ducts. The chemical signals in, say, the odor of another animal's urine, may be analyzed by this special smell gland.

More research is needed to find out how important this secondary sense of smell is in cats and dogs. It may play an important role in sexual and territorial behavior, enabling an animal to detect who left a particular scent mark and what its identity, social rank, sexual status, and emotional state might be. By scent mark, I mean the deposition of some body secretion, like urine, as when a male dog raises its leg or a tomcat sprays. Such marking behavior serves many functions: it is like leaving a calling card telling other animals "I came by here" or "This is my territory." Females mark mainly when they are in heat—the message is obvious. A chemical message, known as a *pheromone*, is passed in the urine at this time and will trigger a male into immediate sexual readiness.

Often a cat or dog that suddenly becomes unhousebroken is simply marking its territory indoors because it is emotionally disturbed. It may feel threatened by a rival next door, or by a change in the home environment, such as the addition of a new pet or loss of one owner. Wild cats assiduously cover their droppings near their dens, but they leave them exposed as signposts at the boundaries of their territory. So your cat may deposit in conspicuous places in the house because it is emotionally disturbed. Dogs will often do this out of spite after being disciplined.

Scent marking is not restricted to urine and feces. Both cats and dogs have scent glands on various parts of the body that play an important role in their social behavior. You must have noticed how a friendly cat rubs its owner with its head. On either side of the head, in front of and below the ears, is a gland; the cat is branding its owner. Other glands are located on the lips and tail, and cats mark furniture by wiping their lips and tails along as they walk by.

Cats that are friendly mark each other with their odors. It is amazing to see what can happen when this "mark of familiarity" is altered. Frequently one cat that has lived for years on very friendly terms with another is attacked when it returns from the veterinarian. Attacks occur especially when the cat's odor has been changed by a skin medication,

Dogs often scrape the ground after marking a tree with their urine. This scraping is not a rudimentary catlike form of burying waste, it adds a visual signal to the scent mark. Raking up the ground, like a leopard scraping a tree with its claws after spraying against the trunk, leaves an impressive additional signal.

I have frequently seen a pair of dogs, male and female, traveling together. After the female urinates the male will mark over the same spot. This may well signal to other dogs, "We are together."

A dog's tendency to roll in foul-smelling things is certainly one of its most deeply ingrained traits—and one of the hardest to eradicate. In spite of punishment, even hosing with cold water, dogs persist in this behavior. I believe they do it for two reasons. First, they may have an esthetic appreciation for some smells, just as we, a more visual species, like bright colors and attractive designs. For reasons similar to our own, a dog may enjoy "wearing" a strong novel odor. The other possibility is that the dog is enhancing its identity, gaining the rewards of the attentions and investigations all over of other dogs.

It is surprising how much time each member of a group of dogs caged together—who therefore know each other intimately—spends in sniffing the others. This kind of social investigation—to sniff and to be sniffed—is one form of social interaction that is extremely difficult for us to comprehend. If we had better noses and used them more in social contexts, this aspect of canine behavior might be easier for us to understand. But the extensive use of deodorants today seems to indicate that, in this culture at least, we try to switch off our noses and mask individual odors with "standard" smells in social contexts, where natural body odors are interpreted as unclean or otherwise objectionable. There are marked cultural differences in the acceptability of body odors. It is said that some Arabs can tell if a person is bad-tempered (sour) or pleasant (sweet) by his or her smell! Perhaps with perfumes we may mask how we feel (although some musk-containing perfumes are sexual

Two fox terriers in the show ring show obvious interest a
leaves his mark. Normally the others would go over, sni
and probably add a little of their own urine to it—an intri
ritual in the world of smell.

or when the cat has gotten out and mingled with ot
It is possible that in marking their territories
cats gain a psychological advantage, making all
into their territories subordinate. Research with ra
shown that the weaker male of a pair will become
if its feces are placed in the test enclosure before t
put together. A buck rabbit will also spray his
with his urine to give them "his mark," much l
marking a companion with its head glands.

Using a model, dogs respond socially, investigating those body parts which normally produce various odors, including mouth, lips, ears, genitals, and anus.

signals). Most female mammals, including women, produce
very specific olfactory signals capable of sexually arousing
the male. If a male chimpanzee's nose is plugged, he will
show no interest in a soliciting female. Interestingly, in the
human female there is an increased sensitivity during men-
struation to a number of odors.

I have often wondered what odors link the mother and infant and help establish their bond. Infant dogs, rats, mice,
and kittens may become imprinted onto the smell of their
mothers—in the cat possibly even to a particular teat. The
mother, too, must become imprinted onto the odor of her
offspring. You may notice how sweet a young kitten or puppy smells and that its breath has a yeasty or fresh-bread
smell. As they mature, these odors disappear. Like the
plumage of many immature birds, these smells may stop
adult animals from responding aggressively; more research
is needed to verify this possibility.

Wolves and foxes have a gland on the tail which smells
like a mixture of violets and fresh-mown hay. Its behavioral
significance is not known. A contrasting sour-smelling
gland under the tail of a cat or dog, situated on either side of
the anus, is better understood. A rancid, sour odor is produced when the animal is alarmed or afraid. This may be an
important alarm or warning signal to companions.

More research will surely be done in the near future on
this fascinating aspect of an animal's world. We know that
salmons and salamanders are able to migrate and find their
way back to their natal waters to reproduce because they
are imprinted to the characteristic chemical odors of their
home waters. We know, too, that some odors may be used
to control animals or to keep insects away from crops. As
of yet we have not discovered the ideal chemicals to keep
coyotes away from sheep or stop the domestic cat or dog
from urinating on furniture. The day may come when we
will use a chemical signal that will stop a dog from attacking

or will make some wild animals lose their fear of us. Until then, castrating our tomcats will stop many of them from spraying and spaying our bitches will keep them from signalling male dogs with their urine when they are in heat.

But the next time you deodorize yourself and put on perfume or after-shave lotion—think twice. It may be more real, if not more beautiful (certainly less confusing to animals) to smell natural. And if you do smell sour, check your diet and your emotions and don't mask the truth with perfume or deodorant. You may trick someone else's nose, but deep down, the body never lies!

8

How Much Does Your Pet Really Know?

WHAT IS SUPPOSED to set us apart from animals is the human mind. An animal knows; a man knows that he knows. But how clear-cut is this division between man and beast?

In the process of evolution, we often find in less evolved forms the rudiments or simple antecedents of more complex, highly evolved structures. It follows, then, that we should find some rudiments of humanlike thinking in animals, and especially in pets that have had long exposure to human beings.

Consider the two-and-a-half-year-old St. Louis mongrel Killer. He outthought his mistress, an experienced dog trainer, and beat her at her own game. Being a curious woman, she decided to tease Killer. Whenever she put on her coat, he would get excited, all ready to go out. So one day she put on her coat and, when Killer got excited, took it off and sat down. After the second time she did this, Killer seemed more subdued; on the third time she opened the door and went out with him.

But he was limping badly on his left front paw. She took him back indoors, laid him on his side, and carefully checked his feet, but found nothing wrong. Suddenly Killer leaped up, tail wagging, eyes gleaming, and wearing the biggest grin on his face that she'd ever seen. He had tricked her!

This will sound farfetched to some. They might argue that a flint or other object might have been stuck in his paws and fell out just before he returned indoors. That isn't impossible, but I do know that dogs will pretend to be lame in order to get attention. The first scientific paper I wrote on this topic over ten years ago was ridiculed by some older, more anthropocentric veterinary colleagues. Since they are closer to animals in their daily lives than most people, I anticipate even more skepticism from the general public.

Perhaps I'm wrong here, and the public finds nothing amazing about Killer showing his owner he understood the strategy of her game. Nothing amazing because, with the trick filming and narrative of some atrociously anthropomorphic Walt Disney animal films and TV's Lassie, our children are taught that animals are just people with fur, thinking and reacting as we do. This is just as wrong as maintaining that animals have nothing in common with the higher qualities of the human species, such as altruism, humor, foresight, and insight.

Diablo, one of my hand-raised coyotes, who now lives in a large outdoor cage in Colorado, uses *bait* to catch prey. He deliberately spreads his dry dog food on the ground and then hides among the rocks in his enclosure until birds fly in. They aren't too difficult to catch because in their panic they fly against the wires of the cage and give Diablo enough time to catch them.

I received a letter the other day from a lady who has one cat that delights in repeatedly scaring a companion cat of lesser intelligence. The "bomber" waits until the other cat is just by the table, then it pushes whatever object it can over the edge at its poor victim!

A photographer friend of mine has a poodle. The dog, whenever severely reprimanded or thwarted, defecates on her owners' bed—on the master's side of the bed, mind you, not on her more permissive mistress's side!

Many readers know how a dog will communicate its desire to go for a walk by bringing its leash to its owner's feet, or will respond eagerly to "Let's go out" or "Where's your leash?"

How much do our pets really know? Perhaps it's a good thing that they can't talk (the stories they could tell!) Sometimes a spark of awareness crosses the incredible void between animal and man, and we are humbled by the depth of understanding of our animal companions. Limited as they are in their nonverbal abilities to communicate, they are far from dumb and unfeeling. Just consider some of the authenticated cases of dogs rescuing people. Such insight and empathy serves to remind us that we are not the only intelligent beings in this universe.

Studies of wild animals, such as wolves, destroy myths of inborn savagery. Wolves are exemplary parents; they, and other social animals such as dolphins and elephants, demonstrate some of the highest qualities—love, empathy, and altruism. With such knowledge, we must come to respect our animal kin. And we must develop a close kinship with animals as well as a reverence for all life if we are to conserve all that is wild and beautiful in this world. We can begin by understanding our pets and appreciating them for what they are: not just dumb, dependent beasts, but creatures that, like little children, cannot communicate with us by words alone.

Although we can learn a great deal about animal behavior in the laboratory and field, what goes on in the special environment of the home, with its close relationships, is often unique and impossible to replicate experimentally in the lab. Who could replicate the case of a Pekingese, an indulged "child substitute," which developed a paralysis in both hind legs when its mistress had a real baby? Greyfriars Bobby, the nineteenth-century Skye terrier whose fidelity became a legend, never left his master. Even when Auld Jock was dead and buried, Bobby slept each night on his grave, for fourteen years. The little dog's devotion is commemorated by a bronze statue and drinking fountain for thirsty animals.

The following anecdote from an observant dog owner shows clearly how, in the selection and arranged breeding for particular traits in different breeds, some characteristics persist for generations, even in dogs no longer worked or occupied in using their "specialist" abilities. She had two such specialists; one a Schipperke, a breed originally developed in Holland to hunt and kill rats on barges. Even today they are superinquisitive, poking their noses into every corner. Her other dog was a Shetland sheep dog, originally bred to protect sheep. Although probably not differing in basic intelligence, these two dogs reacted very differently to an accident in the home. A pet hamster's cage was knocked over accidentally by one of the children. Immediately the Schipperke rushed at it, following his instinct to kill. The sheltie intercepted her companion and protected the hamster, following her strong inborn protective instinct! The hamster was "hers"—just like her human companions of the household.

This anecdote illustrates how man's influence in developing particular attributes in various dog breeds has had a remarkable effect on how a dog will "think" and react.

Olaf Stapleton's science-fiction novel *Sirius*, the story of an experimental dog given the mind of a man, captures the pathos of the unique animal's terrible loneliness. This fiction might be not as far from the truth as we might think.

We are not alone in this vast universe. Although animals do not have human minds, we must thank our pets for giving us something more than companionship. Being with them, we know that we are not alone, that we are not the only thinking and feeling beings.

There are innumerable reports of animal heroism, ranging from the cat that wakes the sleeping houshold in time to allow them to escape from a burning house to the dog that kept his little master away from a rattlesnake and nearly died himself from the bite he received. Some of these are in fact authentic cases of real insightful behavior, animal heroism, and altruism. Many are coincidence: a dog will bark because it is alarmed by smoke and without conscious intention warns its sleeping owners.

Many popular animal programs on TV (like "Lassie" and "Daktari") show trained animals doing simple tricks; they are made to seem like incredible feats within the context of the cleverly edited and spliced film. Probably because of this, people often read too much human sentiment and intelligence into the actions and reactions of their pets. A person living alone, in very close relationship with one or more pets, may well live on a *reciprocal* level of understanding and communication with the animal, well beyond the usual man-animal relationship. The pet living in so close a bond with a human, together with hundreds of hours of indulgent and patient training, could well exhibit above-average potentials and attributes. "My dog talks to me," or "My cat knows everything I say and always knows how I feel," may not simply be the utterances of dotty, eccentric recluses.

The day may come when a pet does hold a deep and meaningful conversation with its owner. We must keep our minds open to this possibility, tempering our impatience and curiosity with healthy skepticism and scientific objectivity.

Many plants seem to respond to certain human "vibrations" (or soothing music). It is only a matter of time, perhaps, before we will respond to them in emotional-psychic ways—and with other living things, too. Perhaps we can begin to learn this sort of communication today from our pets. They, naturally, are more tangible to most of us than plants in their sharing of affection and in their understanding of us. It often exceeds our awareness of them—and of ourselves as well!

If you have an interesting anecdote about your pet, please send me a letter.

9

Touch and Love—Why Pets (and Children) Need Contact

A FEW YEARS ago, child psychiatrist René Spitz discovered that without sufficient love, orphanage infants are prone to infections. Because they do not digest their food adequately their growth may be retarded; they may even develop a wasting disease known as *marasmus.*

He instituted a simple but effective program: handling. The babies were picked up, carried, rocked, and fondled. This was all that they needed. Love without such handling was ineffectual. An infant needs the stimulation of body contact. A baby monkey, separated from its mother, will curl up, clasp itself, and rock to and fro in place of the intimate contact provided by its mother. Even adult humans, will, under stress, clasp themselves and rock to and fro. With prolonged maternal deprivation the infant monkey comes to rely on itself for comfort and gradually becomes so introverted that its social behavior later in life is severely impaired. Sensory- and affection-deprived children may similarly become self-sufficient, introverted, and undemonstrative.

Puppies raised in separate cages may develop signs not unlike those recognized in orphan children by Dr. Spitz, and also usually respond positively when handled by a caretaker.

If deprived of touch—of licking, grooming, rocking, stroking—young animals do not thrive. Why is it that if given this stimulation by a caretaker (who need not feel love toward the infant), all will be well?

Recent studies of human infants and puppies show that gentle rhythmic touching has a profound effect on the physiological functions of the body. Relaxation, salivation, slowing of the heart rate, and peristalsis (increased flow of digestive juices and of digestive movements) occur. It appears that this stimulation, normally provided by the mother, is vital for early development. With time, it becomes associated with pleasure and a bond of affection develops between parent and infant. Prior to this time, though, the bond on the part of the infant is primarily one of physiological dependency: Food (milk) alone is not enough, and love alone (without contact) is insufficient. Dr. H. Harlow has shown that infant monkeys prefer a dummy mother that gives pleasant tactile stimulation but no milk to an all-wire one that gives milk.

Petting or grooming an adult dog or cat produces similar physiological changes, including the slowing of the heart rate and body relaxation. Some cats will even "regress" and behave like kittens, salivating and kneading with their forepaws as though they were nursing.

Fully grown mammals enjoy being groomed or licked by a companion, and will often solicit such touching with a specific display. Monkeys groom each other (they are not picking fleas off), which sometimes serves to reduce tension in the troop. After a fight or a scare they usually groom each other.

Sometimes between adults grooming serves to cement together and maintain a mating or friendship bond. A male red fox will spend hours grooming his mate, and vice versa. My two neutered house cats enjoy grooming each other, often before or after a bout of playful fighting. Sometimes,

An infant rhesus monkey, separated from its mother, shows obvious signs of distress and separation depression.

Social grooming in chimpanzees—hours a day will be spent in this pleasurable pastime. *(S. Halperin)*

between bites, one will briefly lick the other as though to say, "It's OK."

One monkey approaching another will signal its friendly intentions by smacking its lips; a dog does the same by repeatedly extruding its tongue. Both of these signals are derived from grooming actions.

I have seen and heard about abnormal self-grooming in a number of adult animals separated from their companions. Having no one to groom, no way to touch another or to be touched, a baboon in one zoo went crazy and pulled out all its hair. In other zoos, a puma licked a hole in its flank and a brown bear eventually eviscerated itself. Dogs and cats, caged alone for hospitalization or while their owners are on vacation, may lick a paw, knee, or flank raw. Boredom may be a factor, but a lack of loving contact is the most logical underlying cause. The animal tries to compensate for this by stimulating itself, often to the point of mutilation. I have seen the same thing in socially deprived, institutionalized mental patients. If you saw *Fahrenheit 451* you may recall the people of that cold society rubbing and stroking themselves in the subway train.

The need for contact—touch by—with another, seems to be a very basic need in both infant and adult mammals. Give your children and young pets lots of physical contact! It is more significant than words; touch does more than looks or words can. Early deprivation may lead to fear or shyness about touching others and being touched. Hives, urticaria, and other skin rashes are often psychosomatically linked with emotional conflicts involving closeness and the avoidance of others. The skin is an important sense organ for the emotions; many dermatological problems in pets, and especially people, are of psychosomatic origin. No matter how we may try to cover up inside, the body never lies.

Destroying myths of savagery, a mother wolf gently grooms one of her cubs and regurgitates meat for her litter to eat. The more social mammals—wolves, whales, and apes—show strong ties of allegiance to family and care and affection for young.

Get your pet used to your grooming and fondling. With a child, why not try gentle massage of the scalp, back, and feet? Some parents may feel inhibited because touch in our culture is associated primarily with sex. Part of growing up involves escaping the restraints and limitations imposed by the mores of the culture: give your children a chance! Mine, ages nine and twelve, are excellent little masseurs. They enjoy giving and receiving massages, and there's no better way to relieve headache or tension in the shoulders and lower back. As a member of the American Association of Massage Therapists, I speak with experience and conviction.

But you can't touch or massage just anyone, nor can you pet any animal. Some animals, when they mature, need very little contact and often avoid close physical contact with each other, like porcupines (for obvious reasons) and adult lynx and fox (except during the breeding season). Others, like baboons and squirrel monkeys, stay together all the time and derive great pleasure from frequent body contact.

People from different cultures vary in the degree of body contact considered permissible. In some cultures it is acceptable to touch certain parts, even of a stranger's body, which it is taboo to touch in this country. Anyone who has traveled in Italy or South America will know what I mean! Such cultural differences may stem from subtle differences in the way in which infants are handled by their mothers.

I have seen how a wild animal, unsocialized to people, cringes and cowers when it is touched. The contact may even be actually painful. Such states of hyperesthesia, where what would normally be pleasant skin contact is subjectively experienced as extremely painful, also occurs in man in hysterical states. My friend Desmond Morris refers in *The Naked Ape* to what he calls "grooming ailments," the attention-seeking aches and pains of people who require the attention and comfort of others. In a more extreme form these may become the conversion hysterias of neurotics, such as the paralysis of a limb or a phobia about dirt on

Social grooming in baboon and man not only fulfills a hygienic function but also helps establish and maintain close social bonds.

the skin. Perhaps more touch, love and security in infancy could prevent such extreme reactions; such reactions confirm the fact that touch is just as basic a requirement for humans as it is for our fellow animals. A sheep dog will work all day just for a pat or two from its master; a cat will go almost into a trance when its solicitations are rewarded by caresses.

Interestingly, the act of stroking has a soothing effect on the one who is stroking too. I have seen countless performers on TV nervously stroking themselves, or fondling an animal if they are on with one at the time. Executives soothe themselves with smooth worry beads, or run their hands through a teak box of white sand on their desk. Yes, there is feedback from touching, from rhythmically stroking, giving mutual satisfaction to groomer and groomee alike. And the mother and her offspring derive intense enjoyment from doing what is natural and inborn.

One final point—gently stroking a pregnant rat will make her offspring more docile and easier to handle (even if she is separated from them when they are born and the pups are placed with a nonhandled foster mother rat). I know of no corresponding studies on other mammals, but I am sure that this has been unwittingly practiced by man for thousands of years. Practiced since man first began to domesticate animals: he would naturally be gentle and indulge a semidomesticated wolf-dog or cat that was to bear offspring.

So reach out and touch and be touched! It is the essence of being both animal and human.

10

Parents and Pet Owners and Why Your Pet (Child) Misbehaves

CAN YOU RAISE a cat to be like a dog? Does your dog think he's human?

Many people raise their cats from kittenhood with the impression that cats are basically aloof and not very sociable. Their cats usually mature to be aloof and distant: a self-fulfilling prophecy. It could have been different, however. My two cats, Sam, an Abyssinian, and Mocha, a Burmese queen, are both supersociable and surprise many house guests with their friendliness and open curiosity. An elderly friend of mine who raised one of my Chihuahua pups claims that it thinks it is human and will have nothing to do with other dogs—there seems no chance of its ever having puppies, unless they are half human!

The way we raise our pets inevitably influences their temperaments, sociability, and social preferences as they mature. The same holds true for our children. Most parents treat baby girls differently from baby boys. Of course there are variations. Some girls are "tomboys," especially those with older brothers or male playmates next door. Then there are clinical cases of disturbed parents raising a child as if it were of the opposite sex. Almost as bad for the child is to raise it with the expectation that a little girl must like only "feminine" things; and do we not reward "manly" attributes in a boy, even unconsciously? I see a close similarity in the sex-role stereotyping that we unwittingly condition and reinforce in infants and the expectations with which many people raise their cats.

The so-called "people dogs" are also raised under a set of expectations in which their owners believe their pet to be nothing less than a child on four legs. *Restricted rearing—* when an animal has virtually no contact with its own kind, a puppy raised in an apartment and rarely taken out, having its own balcony toilet or one puppy never allowed to play with other pups because it might get hurt or sick—can have similar consequences. How similar are these situations to the couple with a single, overprotected, peer-deprived child, who at the age of five is like a little professor or precious china-doll woman, preferring the company of adults and having difficulty relating to other children. In Europe, the offspring of aristocracy raised by a "nanny" were deprived almost totally of peer interaction, studying at home with a private tutor rather than being sent to preparatory or boarding school. Fortunately for the adult-identifying child, although it is often a traumatic event, going to school is therapeutically a salvation: peer interaction is an essential growth experience. Dr. Harry Harlow has shown in his experiments with rhesus monkeys that infants must have the opportunity to play with peers to grow up normally; those caged just with their mothers, deprived of peer interaction, have social and sexual problems later in life.

I have raised puppies in temporary isolation from their peers, some for the first eight weeks, some for the first sixteen weeks of life. Eight-week-old pups when they first come together are very excited and soon begin to play. But they haven't learned to control the intensity of their bites. Consequently, the playful interactions rapidly disintegrate into fights. After only three or four days, the pups learn to control their bites and play together for longer periods. I remember my own two children first learning to play with a companion of about the same age. An eighteen-month-old,

A puppy raised only with humans ignores its littermates that have been raised together. Early rearing conditions in dog and human infant alike can have profound and long-lasting effects on later social behavior.

like a puppy, has to learn not to poke or bite his playmate or grab his toy, or his companion will cry or fight back. Deprived of such socialization experiences, no child or animal could grow up to have the normal empathic and socially adapted reactions toward its own age-mates.

Sixteen-week-old pups, which are now too human-attached, manifest only a brief curiosity when first put with other pups, then wander off to play by themselves; sometimes they show fear and don't seem to be able to communicate properly. I have seen the same look of dismay and inability to communicate in half-grown wolves hand raised by people which have had no chance to play with their own kind; severe fights sometimes are the result. Even more tragic is the hand-raised gorilla or chimpanzee at the zoo that is put with its own kind when it is almost mature. Such humanized animals show separation depression—they miss their handlers, and ignore their own kin or show fear and defensive behavior in their presence. Rarely do such animals ever breed.

A few years ago I raised a puppy with a family of kittens. The pup came to prefer the company of cats and was afraid of its own kind. Tests with a mirror showed that it reacted as though it thought that it was a cat too! The kittens, however, gained from the experience of being raised with this puppy and were friendly toward strange pups as well. In a way this broader socialization of the kittens supports the contentions of many educators who believe that raising a child in a neighborhood and/or school with children from different ethnic, cultural, and socioeconomic backgrounds may make them socially more flexible and adaptable as adults. Such broad-based socialization on an international basis could be the key to world peace.

There is much more to raising a child or a pet than meets the eye. It is a common observation that the pet owners often resemble their pets. I know people who look just like their bulldogs, beavers, horses, or basset hounds! Of course, many people bear no resemblance to their pets—just as some parents do not resemble their legitimate children. With humans, while there is a genetic relationship between parents and child, the ways in which the child expresses its emotions and preferences are learned from the parents, rather than being inherited per se. As a parent may internalize an image as to how the child should behave and relate, so the pet owner may have an ideal and "shape" its pet to fit to this inner image. This is where preconceptions and the emotional and psychological needs of the parent or pet owner come in, and profoundly influence how "feminized" the little girl will be, how sociable or aloof the kitten will be, how outgoing the puppy or little boy will be when they mature. What are little girls made of?   sugar and spice and all things nice . . . /What are little boys made of? / slugs and snails and puppy dogs' tails! / How a girl or boy, or dog or cat should behave is determined by the ideals and preconceptions of the parent or owner. It is more difficult even to imagine how a child or young animal *spontaneously* behaves in an ambience of unconditional, expectation-free affection and security. The world is full of "shouldisms." These shouldisms can be crippling to development, just as are some of the shouldisms that parents interject into their own lives as models of how they ought to be as parents, husbands, and wives. Freedom for growth, for full self-expression and self-actualization, comes most easily when there are few shouldisms and expectations. Wildness is controlled freedom; as nature guides, shapes, and nurtures growing things, so parenthood can learn from nature. A growing child or pet will never realize its full potential if raised under either complete control or total freedom. An ambience of unconditional, expectation-free affection and security, with protective, guiding, and nurturing "controlled freedom," is needed to provide the best environment for growth.

How far are we from this ideal today? Women's lib and other consciousness-raising movements are freeing us from the old stereotyped roles that limited us, and, as a result, our children. Like children, pets are good reflections of the well-being of a person and his or her home life. Perhaps

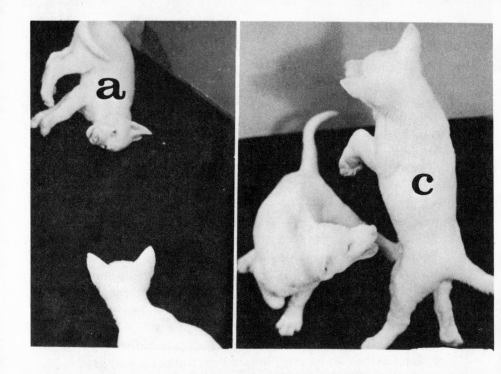

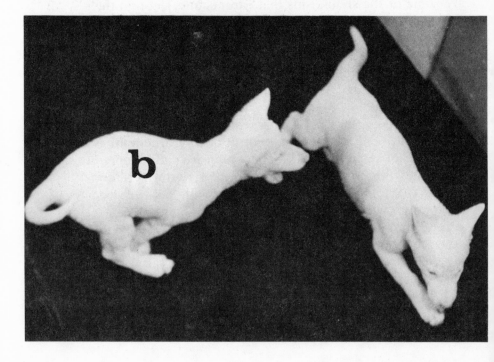

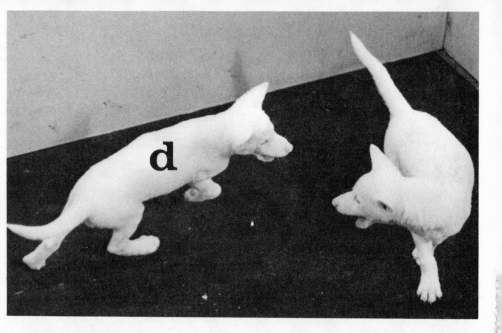

Play—the essence of social learning: Albino dingo dog puppies engage in social play, first giving playful intention signals (a), then chasing, dodging, and playing tag (b-e) . . .

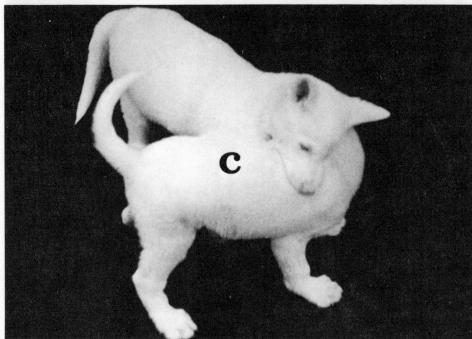

. . . ultimately chasing gives way to wrestling, and actions derived from serious fighting are seen, notably (a) muzzle-, (b) throat-, (c) scruff-, and (d) cheek-oriented bites. The bite is inhibited, however—an aspect of metacommunication and awareness of the nonserious context.

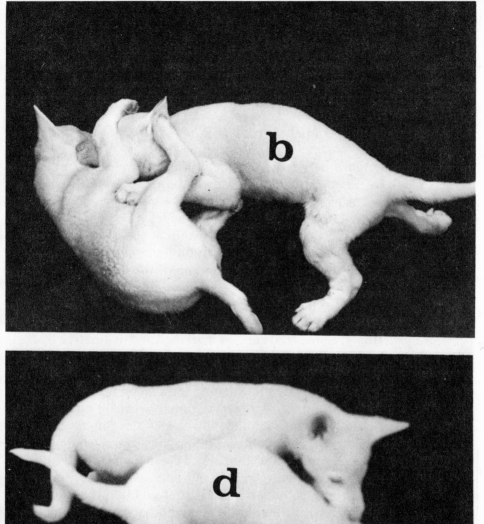

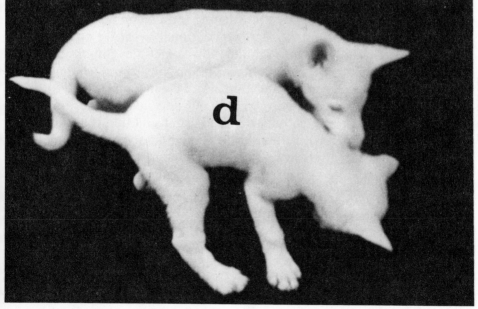

with the increased awareness, the lives of our children and pets will manifest greater fulfillment of the potential so easily stifled by improper and inadequate rearing in early life.

Why Your Pet Misbehaves and What You Can Do About It

There are four basic reasons for a pet or a child to misbehave. By "misbehave," I mean doing something which the owner or parent does not approve of. Immediately we are faced with the issue of socially acceptable behavior relative to the values, needs, and wants of the owner or parent, a one-way judgmental situation that may be improved through empathy and understanding of the pet's or child's behavior.

The first reason to consider is that natural behavior traits or tendencies don't fit in with the owner's life-style or expectations. Some traits are so ingrained and instinctive that the animal literally can not be inhibited from performing these actions: a tomcat spraying furniture, a dog barking excessively, a cat or dog stealing food from the table, or a dog rolling in all kinds of unmentionable smelly odors are all natural behavior and difficult—sometimes impossible— to eradicate. I would put these under the general heading of *natural misbehavior* and animal-human incompatibility.

It is important today to help our pets adapt better to our life-styles, especially in crowded urban and suburban developments. Here, selective breeding for socially desirable temperaments is necessary, for animals with a lesser tendency to bite or bark excessively, those more easily trained and coerced into obedience and conformity. Sometimes surgical operations like spaying and castrating help reduce some of these natural misbehaviors—notably spraying, roaming, and fighting.

It is natural for a child to explore and investigate, occasionally to upset or damage something. A puppy or a kitten is very similar. Young children, in general, are extremely inquisitive and active; this natural behavior should not be inhibited, since it is through this exploratory drive that an animal or child learns about its environment. Far better to protect the child or puppy from potentially dangerous things in the house, like electrical fixtures and ornaments or objects that might fall over and hurt it.

A second reason a pet or a child will misbehave is out of *sheer cussedness*. As a kitten, Sam, my Abyssinian, used to climb on top of a dresser and knock things off, making loud clatterings on the bedroom floor to make me get up and feed him. The category of misbehaving out of sheer cussedness is akin to my third category, in which a pet misbehaves to get *attention*. Here the pet, like many adults, engages in some form of social manipulation in order to get its own way.

A lady wrote to me recently about her cocker spaniel, which gives her painful nips when she engages in conversation with visitors. The dog is nipping her for attention.

A more bizarre case was reported a few years ago by two German veterinarians. They studied a dachshund that for a period suffered from a gastrointestinal disturbance and vomited quite frequently. Medicine resembling paragoric was given to it. Eventually the owners were manipulated into giving the dog a teaspoonful of medicine every evening, otherwise it would refuse to go to sleep. It barked and solicited their attention until it received its medication. The final interpretation of the case was that the pet was addicted to the morphinelike drug. But certainly the attention it received was an important factor in prolonging the treatment.

Another case, also from Germany, involved a dog that developed psychogenic vomiting. This dog also had been sick for a short period of time. During its sickness it learned that as long as it seemed to remain ill it would receive much attention. So, even when it was completely recovered, it continued to vomit. The owner would wake up and give the dog attention in the early hours of the morning. The treatment prescribed: simply to ignore the dog. Within a few days it no longer vomited.

Sometimes I think this kind of manipulation occurs when the pet is left alone for some time. Carpets, drapes, sofa, chairs, and often precious possessions are chewed up. This could be a combination of attention-seeking and sheer cussedness. You should remember that punishment is a form of attention. Some pets, I am sure, develop an almost sadomasochistic relationship with the owner—even painful discipline can be "rewarding." At that time the pet is receiving the undivided attention of its beloved master.

The fourth, and the most important, reason a child or a pet will misbehave is that it is *emotionally disturbed.* Jealousy is a common emotional disturbance. It may be triggered in a child by the birth of a sibling, or in a pet by the introduction of a companion or the birth of a child. The jealousy reaction ranges from sulking, refusal to eat, temper tantrums, destroying the household, nipping the owner, and occasionally biting the newcomer.

One of the most bizarre emotional disturbances I have come across was described by an Austrian veterinary colleague, Dr. Ferdinand Brunner. A dachshund had seizures whenever its owners engaged in a marital squabble. As soon as they left the room, however, the little dog would immediately get up and follow them!

The range and variety of emotional disturbances that dogs may develop is in contrast to the more limited range of symptoms that a disturbed cat manifests. The most usual misbehavior of emotional origin in the cat is suddenly becoming unhousebroken. The cat no longer uses the litter tray and urinates or defecates in all parts of the house. This behavior can persist long after the triggering emotional situation has passed. For example, a new more aggressive and dominant cat in the neighborhood could cause this behavior, or it may be caused by a change in a relationship in the home: the introduction of a new pet, the death of a companion pet, or the death or absence of an owner.

This last category of misbehaviors originating from emotional disturbances is one of the reasons I am "turned off" by the usual dog-training manuals and cat-care books. They do not present enough information to give the owner a closer understanding of the emotional needs of the pet. Discipline and training alone are not enough for a child or a pet. We need to acquire a much deeper empathic level of understanding.

The key to training, discipline, and understanding is patience. When you are communicating with your pet keep your commands simple. A whole volley of words can be confusing. Cats and dogs have a capacity to learn a number of simple commands, such as "down," "sit," "no," and so on. The dog's capacity seems greater, probably because the dog is more dependent than the cat. Cats do not respond naturally to a pack leader. They are solitary animals and so there is a natural biological limitation to the degree of attachment and allegiance they will have with the owner. This also limits their degree of trainability.

On the "Tonight Show" recently, Johnny Carson made the point that he has little or no time for cats because they just sit on top of the television and don't do tricks like a dog. Some people favor a pet that is more other-directed and easily trained. While dogs generally fit this category, not all do. Some breeds, such as the basenji, are catlike in their aloofness and independence. Others, like the shelty and the German shepherd, have been bred to be highly trainable. The more trainable, the less disobedience and misbehavior problems are likely when the animal matures. This is very important with physically powerful dogs. Again, I contend that anybody who has a large dog—a German shepherd, a Saint Bernard, a Doberman pinscher— should have a license to the effect that the owner is a competent handler of such a dog. This would certainly help reduce the number of severe bites and deaths caused by canine sociopaths and delinquents.

It is a thrilling experience to see a well-trained German shepherd in an obedience class perform incredible feats, or a shepherd working with his sheep dog. The eye contact and the communication involved between animal and handler is indeed quite remarkable. Such superdogs are not as rare as one might think.

Dogs have been domesticated for thousands of years and in the process they have been made more dependent. The more dependent the animal is, the more trainable it is.

If we raise a puppy with very little human contact it will not become emotionally bonded to people. Being less dependent, and not so adequately socialized, it will be much harder to train than one with much human contact during its formative weeks. This is one of the problems in buying a dog that has been in a kennel for four or five months or caged in a pet store for a prolonged period, or obtaining one of obscure origin from a humane shelter; a dog that has had a lot of contact with other dogs and inadequate contact with people is one that will misbehave. Being less emotionally dependent he will be less concerned with pleasing his master. The key to trainability is an emotional link of dependency and affection, and not intelligence per se.

An important link between animal and man and between man and man is eye contact. A direct stare is a form of asserting dominance. Before you give a command to your pet, establish eye contact. Then give the verbal command. With a dog this may be facilitated in various situations with a choke chain and a long leash.

Cats can also be leash trained, but this is not usually the situation. One way of controlling a cat over a distance is with a water pistol. Establish eye contact, make your command—"down," "no." A quick squirt will get the cat down off the dresser or from among the precious plants on the windows in no time at all.

Some varieties of cat are more dependent than others. The Siamese is the most trainable. You can easily teach the cat to walk on a leash or retrieve things, and in my experience they have a far better comprehension of verbal commands than the average alley cat. Of course, there are always exceptions.

You must be consistent in giving reward or punishment. *Always.* Inconsistency leads to confusion. Under such confused circumstances the pet may, like a child, begin to manipulate, to solicit your attention and affection, and get away with its mischief. I remember one elderly couple who had a large German shepherd with which they had problems. The dog would not obey a single command unless it felt like responding. This dog was literally "number one" in the household, and in many ways resembled a human adolescent delinquent. Because the owner is not seen as the pack leader, such pets easily take over a household; because of overpermissive and overindulgent rearing they can become psychopathic to the extent that they have no inhibitions about biting people to get their own way.

As young male dogs mature they go through an adolescent crisis before they reach full sexual maturity. At this time they often test the owner, and if they can intimidate their master they may obtain the upper hand psychologically and win this dominance fight. From then on it is a quick road downhill. The relationship has been turned upside down and the dog is Number one in the household; everyone has to accede to its every whim and fancy.

It has been said by some authorities that it is impossible to discipline a cat, that a cat has no conscience. I would say that it is possible to effect inhibitory training in a cat and that a cat does have a sense of right and wrong. But a cat doesn't express its conscience to the same degree as a dog. We know that the dog has done something wrong when we come home and, instead of greeting us, it slinks under the table. The cat, however, doesn't manifest this kind of behavior, unless, of course, it was terrified by the crash of the plant pot or lamp that it upset during your absence.

People will often discipline their pet for misbehavior, not understanding fully that the animal was simply doing what comes naturally. For example, a young woman wrote recently that she felt embarrassed when her dog greeted her and urinated submissively because it looked to others as though she mistreated it. She tried punishing the dog,

shouting at it and picking it up by the scruff of the neck—
only making the dog urinate more.

Another inappropriate form of discipline is chastising a
dog after it has run away and been caught. Punishing a dog
when it comes back to you is no way to get it to stay with
you! When an owner has chased a dog halfway around the
neighborhood trying to catch it, a reward should be given,
rather than punishment. But at such times it *is* difficult to
keep one's cool!

Although declawing is one way of handling the cat that
misbehaves and ruins the furniture and carpets, trimming
the claws is a more humane alternative. You might also
consider remotivating the animal to give it something else
to do in such cases—a toy to chase or pounce on and
"kill." Or give it a scratching post, made simply of a strip
of carpet, perhaps with a little catnip underneath.

In conclusion, then, I would say that there are many
cases of pets being deliberately disobedient out of sheer
cussedness, or in order to manipulate the owner to get his
attention. If we do not understand the natural behavior of
our pets, much of what they do may be misinterpreted as
undesirable behavior. Here a closer understanding of the
needs and wants of the pet is of immense value.

It is depressing and infuriating to hear some of the re-
marks that people make when they hand their cats or dogs
in for adoption or destruction at the humane society. Reasons given: it barks too much; or it sheds; or it's too much
trouble—it has to be taken out on a leash too often. Many
such people would be much better off with potted plants,
preferably thorny cacti! Sensitive pets do not behave like
vegetables and yet their owners expect them to conform
and be unobtrusive at all times.

Continued enjoyment, however, can come from a deeper
understanding of the nature of our pets. The average cat or
dog is not just a dumb animal. Too often it just does not understand *precisely* what the owner wants. We have an obligation to learn to understand our pets far better than we
have done so far. Many abstract, esoteric school science

programs would benefit by the inclusion of something more relevant and more accessible—a study of the growth, personality, behavior, and habits of a child's pet or of the animals in the neighborhood.

Do animals in the wild ever misbehave? "Misbehavior" is a value judgment. It is based on a consensus of what is socially acceptable and unacceptable. Certainly in a wolf pack, a low-ranking older animal that gets out of line will be disciplined, while a young cub will be indulged and allowed much more leeway. Very often I see a wolf or dog using playful gestures as a way of circumventing and manipulating a higher-ranking animal; but the higher-ranking one knows the game and sometimes goes along with it.

A child has to grow up and learn what he can and cannot do in society. He learns this from his parents and especially from his peers at school. A puppy or kitten's experiences with its litter mates are no less critical in influencing later social behavior toward its own kind. A young dog confined indoors all day is like a energetic child confined behind its desk all day and forced to do its studies. This is no way to raise a young creature. Options must be provided to allow potential to develop through wide experience. This is the way to raise children and pets: in an ambience of unconditional affection and consistent discipline, leading to self-control and awareness.

11

Neuroses in Dogs

TO A REMARKABLE degree, the evolution of the dog has accompanied human cultural evolution. Some ten thousand years ago, when *Canis familiaris* first moved close to man's campfires, it, like man, lived largely a hunting and scavenging existence, serving man by warning of the presence of large animals and possibly learning to bring down game on command. With the development of pastoral society a thousand or so years later, man and dog learned to tend flocks of sheep and goats and to protect homesteads. At the same time society began to stratify. Small elite classes emerged, composed of aristocrats who, for the first time, could afford to keep nonworking animals. These prehistoric pet fanciers learned surprisingly subtle techniques of genetic engineering, developing such extraordinary canine mutants as the papillons and Pekingeselike creatures that appear on Etruscan vases and in Grecian friezes.

Throughout European history pets carried much the same social significance as did clothes or dwellings. A peasant, for example, was not allowed to have a pet above his social station, such as a coach dog, lapdog, or falcon. These were exclusively for the aristocracy. In fact, the peasant could usually not afford to feed a nonproductive pet.

People keep dogs these days for a few old reasons and a lot of new ones. Status is still heavily involved. In the southern United States a good coon hound will fetch as much as two thousand—an amount wildly beyond any realistic economic assessment of what the dog does for the master. Rather, the dog represents for the owner a ticket into an elite group of hound owners as well as a Freudian projection of his own ego. Many dogs fulfill the desires of frustrated masters, representing power, aggression, sexual freedom, virility. A small man is often seen with a mastiff or Great Dane. A fierce dog on the end of a leash often reinforces the owner's confidence as would any other weapon.

Dogs must now substitute for both concrete and abstract aspects of human experience that we are often denied by modern modes of living. A Greenwich Village photographer acknowledges that his Airedale provides a link with nature and makes him feel more authentic, less anonymous in the confines of New York concrete. A dog in the home provides many of us with someone to come home to—reliable, accepting, trusting. Dogs are honest, existential, living only for the moment. When we receive an enthusiastic canine greeting, we trust its sincerity. A dog may be a confidant for a lonely child or a link to an often absent father through joint training and exercising of the animal. Some child psychologists are now using dogs (called canine cotherapists) in hospitals. They find that a child who doesn't relate to peers or parents may trust a dog, which he finds loving, accepting, and reliable. The therapist can often talk to the child about the dog; and, once this first bond is established, it may lead to a stronger bond with humans.

To fulfill such ends, man has to a considerable extent remade dogs in his own image. He has selectively bred, for example, dogs with a babyish appearance—pugs, Chihuahuas, Pekingese—that elicit human parental responses. Many of the most popular dogs exhibit the "Peter Pan syndrome," or neoteny, remaining docile, dependent, and perpetual puppies throughout their lives. Such dogs commonly serve as child substitutes for childless couples and singles.

One of my graduate students and his wife who do not plan to have children recently adopted a dog from the humane society for the conscious purpose of absorbing their unused parental affection.

We expect, of course, that such a dog can absorb all this affection without becoming spoiled—an almost impossible demand. With an abruptness unheard of on an ordinary evolutionary time scale, we are asking dogs to change from fierce hunters and protectors into docile groupies willing to accept any stranger, tolerate children, and ignore cats. We expect them to allow the repeated invasion of their territory by mailmen and meter readers. After breeding dogs to be sexually promiscuous and early to mature (to facilitate further selective breeding), we then ask them to live a life of nearly total celibacy.

On a longer-term basis our obsession with dog shows is resulting in genetic changes that are harming many breeds. Constant inbreeding to achieve exaggerated characteristics—long noses, short noses, low hips, short legs—encourages increasing mutations toward brachycephaly (round heads), achondroplasia (short limbs), retinal blindness, floating kneecaps, and dwarfism. We breed for show gazellelike Irish setters that could never be used in the field, as are their heavy-boned, working counterparts. Spaniels and retrievers that look graceful in the ring are, like as not, virtual zombies prone to posing immobile for hours and retaining none of their old work habits.

The growing custom of using dogs to accommodate human needs often results in turnabout demands by the dogs themselves. After one woman brought her dog into New York's Animal Medical Hospital for expensive orthopedic surgery, the staff found that it refused to eat from a bowl. They called the woman, who replied that at home she always seated her dog in a chair and fed it with a spoon. A woman staffer at the hospital tried this routine and had no further trouble. Such canine problems, of course, merely offer lonely masters the opportunity to bestow more affection or worry upon their charges. As a result of canine

Sexlike mounting in the dog, as in the baboon, may occasionally be a way of asserting dominance. Note submissive expression of dog in background. Two male dogs (below) engage in homosexual pairing without intromission. This "affair" lasted for one day and the dog on top prevented any other dog from coming near. The "mountee," although tired, showed no obvious displeasure!

neoteny created by selective breeding and overindulgence, domestic dogs are losing the resilience they once had. We carried out comparison studies between lab-raised beagles and Chihuahuas, two rather neotenic breeds, and coyotes, wolves, and jackals. Members of each breed were left in isolation for several hours. The beagles and Chihuahuas urinated, defecated, and cried constantly, but the wild species seemed unaffected.

Fritz Perls, founder of Gestalt therapy, noted that most behavioral disorders in man are related to one form of dependency or another, such as fear of rejection, jealousy, and immature dependence upon external support or sanction. Similarly, in the dog, a threat to, or disturbance of, the relationship with the owner may be the cause of several disorders. This is especially evident in overindulged and overdependent dogs, particularly of the more infantile breeds.

Owners who work during the day put special stress on their pet. The dog—bred to need companionship and then abandoned most of the time—is caught in a double bind. The commonest reaction is destruction of household objects, such as furniture, books, clothes, and especially objects the owner prizes, such as a pipe or slipper. When the owner comes home, the lonely dog may overreact, greeting him excessively, racing from room to room and urinating uncontrollably (a sign of submission). When the owner of one Dalmatian leaves the house, the dog carefully opens every door, then races to the bedroom and removes the heirloom bed cover—without ripping it. Then, on the woman's side of the bed, it digs a hole to await her return (she pays the dog more attention than does her husband). One day the frustrated dog dug all the way to the springs and then buried a banana in the hole.

When they have grown accustomed to being the center of attention, dogs often inhibit normal human emotional relationships. Several situations are especially common. Many girls will go out with a boy only if their dog likes him. Emotional triangle problems often involve a dog's jealousy of a boyfriend, who may even be attacked. This is a special dan-

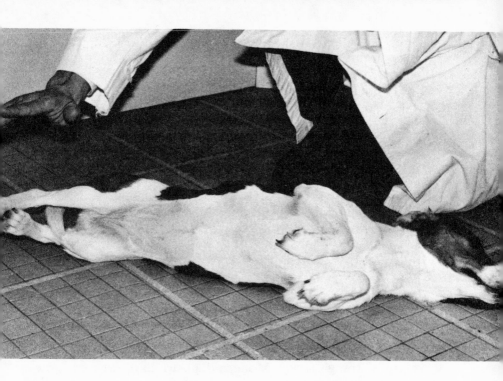

A beagle from an extremely timid line "freezes" in catatonia when gently placed on its side. In a comparable way, a frog is "hypnotized," or, more correctly, put into a state of tonic immobility, when placed on its back.

ger in this age of crime consciousness, when so many girls
have attack-trained guard dogs. One girl, who owned a jealous cocker spaniel, got married and subsequently found
that her dog would lie in wait behind the sofa for her new
husband, attacking him every time he came into the house.
I recommended that before kissing her husband she kiss the
dog, and the problem was solved. I receive several calls a
year from baffled husbands who are forced to sleep on the
sofa because their wives are under constant guard.

Spoiled bitches—especially those accustomed to sleeping
on the owners' bed—may suffer acutely if they become
pregnant. If they are banished to the cellar as delivery time
approaches, gestation may be prolonged due to psychological stress. They may do nothing to assist the births or to remove fetal membranes, and so the owner must help out.

Suppressed urges in dogs result in a whole panoply of
odd behavior. Most canids, for example, customarily use
urination for territorial marking and urinate whenever they
find a strange scent. Modern dogs are hard pressed, however, to respond to the myriad signals they may encounter
in crowded neighborhoods and may urinate (or try to) as
many as two hundred times during an evening walk. If
nothing else, this behavior may be leading to an unprece-
dented degree of sphincter control.

The boredom of human-imposed confinement weighs
heavily on dogs. Compulsive neurotic pacing is common
among zoo animals confined to small spaces. When dogs
have companionship, on the other hand, the size of the
space they live in seems less important. Modern dogs may
feel the need to mark their territory indoors as well as out.

When we do not allow females in heat to mate, they may
not only go through realistic pseudopregnancies, complete
with lactation and swelling, but also displacement behavior
that is almost fetishistic. The bitch may adopt a slipper as a
phantom puppy and guard it fiercely in a nest of fallen
clothes.

One way to soften the isolation of lone dogs, when it is
impossible to provide a canine companion, is with another

This young dog has an erection as it is talked to and petted. Such excitement with people is a perfectly normal arousal phenomenon, not a sexual perversion. In some monkeys and in the hyena it has evolved into a social display.

pet. At times any other living thing seems to satisfy some dogs' craving for a playmate. A girl's overindulged toy poodle had pups, which it did not know how to care for—the owner had to do everything. But since she worked during the day, she had to sell the pups, and the mother began tearing up the house. I gave her a box turtle. As soon as the girl put the turtle down, the dog began licking its backside as though it were a puppy. When the turtle defecated, the dog cleaned up afterward. Then the turtle walked to the dog's dish and ate some food, and the dog responded by trying to nurse the turtle. The turtle/poodle relationship lasted for two beautiful years until the turtle died.

One of the saddest human-induced behavioral disorders found in dogs is kennelosis, or institutionalization syndrome, which seems to result from confinement and lack of stimulation during the critical formative months of puppyhood. When a dog is plunged from a cage into a complex human environment, it commonly suffers a crippling nerve overload and withdraws into a dark corner—both psychically and physically.

A woman who brought a rottweiler wanted to take it from the United States to England, but the dog, at the age of three months, had to be left in quarantine in England for six months. The woman visited the dog every weekend, and, as a result, the dog became well adjusted to people, but, when its sentence was up, it could no longer handle itself outside of its cage. The first day out of confinement it fell down the stairs. The second day it fell out of a station wagon, and after that it refused to come out from under the sink. Only after long treatment with mild tranquilizers and gentle immersion in the real world did the dog begin to shake free of its kennelosis syndrome.

The army's training program for attack dogs was upset temporarily by kennelosis, when the handlers neglected to provide a sufficiently diverse environment for puppies. Although the dog's intelligence was well developed and they were entirely acclimated to people, they freaked out when they first reached a forest, where they would spend most of their adult lives working. The mere rustling of leaves was enough to make some of them defecate in fear. Now the dogs are raised in a sylvan environment from earliest puppyhood.

We have found that those pups given a regular program of stimulation—noise, lights, cold places to walk—become more responsive and adaptable than nonstimulated peers. The second important element is socialization, or abundant early contact with people. This handling must be started by about six weeks of age. Guide dogs' trainers have found that, if socialization is delayed until twelve weeks, learning is so severely inhibited as to make the dog useless for guiding.

We have learned a great deal about raising dogs by watching how a wolf raises its cubs. A wolf mother is extremely affectionate and tolerant toward her cubs—up to a point. When cubs overstep their bounds—by playing too roughly with the mother or wandering away—discipline is immediately enforced by a warning growl, a direct stare, or even a quick nip. The cubs quickly learn the boundaries of permitted behavior and stay within them. At the same time the mother uses even mock violence very sparingly.

The dominant wolf cub in a family of captive wolves managed to kill a rat by himself. His mother came into the cage, obviously wanting the rat herself. She sniffed at it, and the cub responded by growling and snapping. Instead of countering with force, however, she was more subtle. She looked at him for a long time, then went to the corner of the cage, dug up a piece of caribou meat, and dangled it before the pup. The pup leaped at the chunk of caribou, and the mother went back to make a meal of the rat. By not resorting to force, she managed to save his "ego" and showed foresight in manipulating her cub.

Child psychologists tell us that the use of violence condones violence, and we might do well to apply this maxim to our treatment of young dogs. Futhermore, the wolves teach us that, before any discipline can be used, an emotional bond must be established. Up to the age of about eight weeks nothing but "love therapy" should be applied, establishing bonds of trust; only at about twelve weeks should any discipline be used, and then only to establish the outer limits of behavior.

We must also recognize the wide temperamental differences among different breeds of dogs. For timid types, such as beagles and toys, a direct stare or gruff word is usually chastisement enough. Oversevere control can totally dampen the spirit of such dogs. More animated and independent breeds, especially terriers, require—and at times seem to demand—a firmer hand and even occasional force in order to establish dominance. The owner, like the parent wolf, must be "top dog." Overindulgence with either type can result in either social maladjustment similar to that of a bratty child or overdependence verging on helplessness.

Once truly antisocial behavior is established, it may be impossible to curb. To a certain extent, we might again look to wild canids for useful techniques. A mother wolf will seize an unruly cub by the scruff or muzzle and pin him to the ground, which induces an innate submissive response. Touching a dog in the groin area also calms it, and petting reduces the heart rate. If the dog is beyond responding to normal canine signals, drastic means may be required.

While running for the telephone, one owner stepped on his dog and was subsequently bitten each time the phone rang. A trainer put the dog into a kennel and rang random bells in its cage for a solid week. This repeated exposure taught the dog that the sounds were innocuous and desensitized the biting response.

A pediatrician, aghast at the number of children being bitten by dogs, evolved a technique to curb biting. When a dog began to attack a child, she would hang it by the neck for two or three minutes until it nearly passed out. She reported that the biters were immediately cured. R.W. Redding of the University of Alabama reports that frontal leucotomy operations reduce aggression in dogs, and others report success with deep barbiturate anesthesia. Such ex-

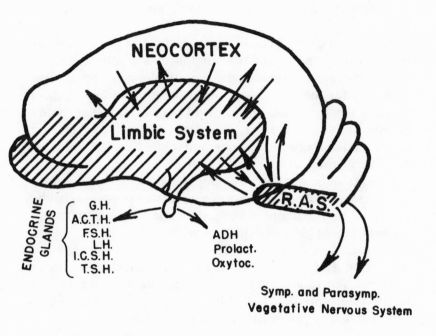

The brain of a dog contains the same basic structures as the human brain: a limbic emotional center, a brain-stem (RAS) arousal system, and a pituitary-gland hormone-control system. The main difference is that man has more neocortex—for speech, memory, fine motor control, and possible conscious control of the lower centers.

treme measures would perhaps be unnecessary if man understood more about dog psychology.

Given the complexity of canine behavioral problems, which are only beginning to be understood, the veterinarian will in the future carry a different—and heavier—responsibility than before. As nutritionally balanced dog foods, better vaccines, and more effective deworming techniques reduce the veterinarian's physical chores, he will be freed for this consultative work. However, veterinarians still receive little formal training in the area of relations between pet and owner.

Finally, dogs are accompanying people in their neuroses not only on a one-to-one basis but also as a population. Although there are no good figures available, it is obvious that there are far too many dogs in this country, many of them running through cities in semiwild packs. However, many people hesitate to sterilize their dogs because of the close identification between owner and pet. New techniques, however, could avert many of these personal crises. Experiments indicate that while puppies may be injected with a permanently sterilizing hormone, female puppies must be sterilized by the adopter when they reach sexual maturity. Typically enough, man and dog seem to be facing this impasse together. A man is reluctant to sterilize either himself or his dog. But, as man and dog have grown steadily closer over the ten thousand years of their companionship, we might safely predict that at least on a technical level this problem will be resolved for both in the near future.

So far as I am aware, there has been no detailed study of the behavior of pets from disturbed homes: homes where a master is a paranoid hypochondriac, obsessive compulsive, or manic depressive; where a child is autistic, hyperactive, or emotionally disturbed; where a mother is schizophrenic or psychotic.

In *Sybil*, the biography of a woman with sixteen separate personalities, the following passage describes how her cat behaved in relation to some of these personalities; namely toward Teddy, Mary, Marcia, and Peggy Lou:

> What Teddy reported with words, Capri, Sybil's cat, revealed through action. Upon "coming to" Sybil became expert in inferring from the cat's behavior which of the other selves had been present. With Mary, Capri was quiet, lovable, wanting to be held and petted. With Marcia, Capri would rub against her face as a gesture of comfort.

But it was with Peggy Lou, in whose presence the cat became frisky, that Capri underwent the most complete transformation. Knowing instinctively that it was Peggy Lou, the cat would race around the apartment and make its frenetic way to Peggy Lou's lap or shoulder. "Nice old cat," Peggy Lou would say, holding the animal a bit too tightly. But Capri didn't mind. The cat, who had no hesitancy about scratching any of the others, wouldn't scratch Peggy Lou.

"Maybe," Sybil quipped, "Capri is multiple too."

BREED	TYPE	LIKES DOGS	LIKES PEOPLE	EMOTIONAL STABILITY	TRAINABILITY	NEED FOR FREEDOM	ONE-MANNISHNESS
Golden Retriever	Sporting	+	++	++	+	+	−
Cocker Spaniel	Sporting	+	+	+	+	+	−
Afghan	Hound	+	±	±	±	++	±
Beagle	Hound	+	++	+	+	+	−
Alaskan Malamute	Working	±	+	+	±	++	±
German Shepherd	Working	±	±	±	++	+	±
Bull Terrier	Terrier	−	++	+	+	+	±
Irish Terrier	Terrier	±	++	+	+	+	−
Yorkshire Terrier	Toy	±	+	+	+	+	−
Poodle	Toy	+	+	±	++	+	−
Bulldog	Nonsporting	±	++	+	+	+	−
Chow-Chow	Nonsporting	±	±	+	+	+	+

− INDICATES ABSENCE OF TRAIT;
+ INDICATES PRESENCE,
++ STRONGLY PRESENT;
± MEANS BEHAVIOR MORE STRONGLY INFLUENCED BY ENVIRONMENT THAN BY GENES.

This cnart is only a general guide to breed behavior. The handling history of an individual dog can change its behavioral characteristics considerably. For example, dogs vary widely according to which kennels they come from. Normally docile cocker spaniels and poodles may turn out to be unstable and vicious if raised in certain kennels.

One-mannishness refers to the preference of some breeds, such as chows, for a single master; others, such as beagles, are less discriminating.

PART II

Other Creatures Wild and Tame

12

The Effects of Domestication on Pets

IT IS HARD to imagine that a tiny Chihuahua and an Irish wolfhound are closely related, or that the placid contented cat curled up by the fireside is a nighttime prowler and killer. These animals are, respectively, the product of some ten and six thousand years of human intervention in their breeding, part of the continuing process known as domestication. Unfortunately, since records are almost nonexistent and archeological remains are few, the details of what domestication has done to the physiology, behavior, and psychology of the cat and dog come only indirectly through studying their wild (undomesticated) relatives. This comparative approach, however, is valid, for both cats and dogs are derived from ancestral species still existing, or from close descendants. The ancestor of the domestic cat is *Felis lybica*, the Kaffir or desert cat. The domestic dog may have more than one progenitor: the Asiatic wolf (*Canis lupus pullipes*) is favored by many; on the other hand, a dingolike "prototype" dog may also be implicated. The latter today is represented by the feral dingo of Australia and the pariah dogs of Asia and North Africa.

Before reviewing some of the consequences of domestication specifically in cats and dogs, an intriguing experiment by Professor D.K. Beylaev from the Siberian Institute, Novosibirsk, should be mentioned. Working with red foxes, he selectively bred the most docile ones for no less than fourteen generations. His findings illustrate some important consequences of domestication; the selected trait (docility) was correlated with other changes that were not deliberately selected.

After the tenth generation, changes were evident in body proportions (eg. head size) and coat color. These docile offspring of docile parents showed a more subdued adrenal response to stress than the wild control subjects; interestingly, the females showed signs of developing a second estrus or heat (the control subjects, like all wild canids, had only one annual heat). Selection for docility thus influenced the adrenal-pituitary and gonadal-pituitary hormonal systems. It also caused a "destabilization" of the genetic makeup, or *genome,* in that new physical types were developed. From this "loosening up" of the physical makeup, new mutations or recombinations could be selected and bred to produce lines with different body proportions, coat type, and so on.

It should be emphasized that *domestication* and *taming,* terms often used synonymously, refer to two distinctly different processes. Taming involves habituation and training, overcoming the fear of man, which may be greatly facilitated by socialization, especially early in life. Socialization is the development of an affectional bond with a member of a larger group, as between parent and infant.

"Gentling," or habituating a relatively wild animal to human contact while pregnant, may result in the offspring being easier to handle. Gentling represents a transitional stage between taming (of one individual) and domestication. This phenomenon has been demonstrated in rats under controlled laboratory conditions.

Domestication is selective breeding for desired qualities plus early socialization—it is thus genetic selection as well as an experiential or learning process. "Domesticated" animals which received no socialization or early taming, may regress and become wild and unapproachable. Such newly wild animals will still produce offspring more easily tamed than those from a wild, nondomestic species. However, if, like the Australian dingo, a once domestic species has been feral for several generations, and therefore subject once again to purely natural selection, the offspring will be feral. Domestication, then, is a process of genetic and experiential (social and environmental) manipulation—a special form of evolution under human direction.

Dogs

Man, in the sense of "directing" the evolution of domestic animals,' has become god. Although he has not quite created the dog in his own image, he has had a more profound influence on this animal than on any other species.

The following comparisons between wild canids and domesticated dogs are drawn primarily from my own studies of hand-raised wolves, jackals, coyotes, dog x wolf, and dog x coyote hybrids.

Most dogs attain sexual maturity by six months of age; the females have two, and sometimes three, estrus cycles annually, and males constantly produce sperm. Dogs are generally sexually promiscuous. Wild canids generally do not attain sexual maturity until one to two years of age; the females only have one annual estrus, males are only seasonally fertile and they show more frequent mate preferences than their promiscuous socialized relatives. Domestication obviously has had a marked effect on canid sexuality.

Wild canids in captivity are generally highly exploratory, more active, and more efficient at attacking and killing prey than many breeds of domesticated dog. The latter manifest bite inhibition (soft mouth) and may even react to live prey, such as rats, as though they were play companions! Domestic dogs are also more trainable; not because they are more intelligent, but because they are more dependent than hand-raised wild species, even when raised and socialized in the same manner.

Wariness of strangers and unfamiliar objects is a common trait of wild canids, along with the instructural flight and critical distance reactions. Such reactions are rare in domesticated dogs and are probably wild traits that were selected against, and so bred out, in the process of early domestication.

Dogs generally accept strangers readily, although this readiness is greatly influenced by early socialization and inheritance—some breeds are naturally more wary than others. Such acceptance reflects a greater capacity to develop secondary social relationships, subsequent to successful socialization in the critical early life period. This capacity is extremely limited in wild canids. Domesticated dogs are also more vocal than wild canids, the multipurpose bark and attention-soliciting yelp being species-typical for *Canis familiaris.*

Domestication may also have caused the persistence of infantile behavioral and physical traits into maturity. This varies from breed to breed, being especially evident in the toy and miniature varieties. Genetic influences are involved as well as early experience; a dog raised as an overdependent "perpetual puppy" may in fact become one.

Selective breeding has contributed to subtle differences between breeds, in such traits as sociability and proximity tolerance. Beagles, for example, are generally gregarious and have a high proximity tolerance. Terriers are less gregarious, show a lower proximity tolerance, and form clear dominance hierarchies in small caged groups.

Breed differences in performance in specific tasks (tracking, retrieving, guarding, etc.) point not to overall differences in intelligence per se, but to "specialist" abilities or roles. Such superior attributes are breed specific; compare, for example, the incredible nose of the bloodhound and the relatively "noseless" gazehound or bird-dog types like the saluki and pointer.

Different breeds have as a consequence of generations of

careful selective breeding, different attributes or inborn specialist abilities. These abilities or traits, being at a low threshold, are more "accessible" to training or environmental shaping; this is a remarkable example of the results of "genetic engineering." Even when raised for a few generations without specific work or training, shepherds will guard, sheep dogs will herd, beagles will follow a rabbit track, and retrievers will retrieve, all with ability and eagerness rare in other nonspecialist breeds or random-bred (mongrel) dogs.

Differences *within* breeds have received little detailed study. Sex differences in certain skills or traits, and behavioral differences associated with different coat colors, await closer investigation and quantification

Persistent traits often considered undesirable in contemporary pet dogs which may be eliminated via rigorous training, deconditioning, or surgery include: relative hypersexuality; excessive barking; marking (urinating) in the house; "hypertrophy" of territorial defensiveness associated with confinement, restraint, or high density of dogs in a neighborhood; roaming; scavenging; chasing "prey" (substitute bicycles, cars, and passersby); nondiscriminatory territorial aggression (attacking mailmen or any other "intruders" or "trespassers"); overprotectiveness of "pack" (children of the house); status-related aggression (rivalry fights with overpermissive owner for dominance); the "socially maladjusted canine sociopath"; pseudo- or phantom pregnancy; overdependence, fear of being left alone (destroys furniture, barks excessively, or defecates and urinates in house); hyperactivity; excessive timidity. With overdependence, often reinforced by the method of rearing, *sexual imprinting* onto man may occur, with subsequent interference with breeding and later maternal behavior. These problems, some of which are more common in one breed, strain, or sex than another, are sometimes enhanced or inhibited by the way in which the dog is raised. (They have been discussed at length in *Understanding Your Dog*.) Selective breeding may be focused more rigorously on some of these problems in the near future to make the dog even more adaptable (and domesticated).

Cats

Cats are basically less gregarious than dogs. In the wild they are a relatively solitary species and domestication seems to have caused only a slight increase in sociability. However, an increase in sociality to the extent that some cats are quite sociable to their own species and especially to man may indicate a trend toward infantilism. Early rearing conditions and optimal socialization, rather than genetic selection, may be the major contributing factor to such behavior.

Prey-killing behavior is absent in many cats. This may reflect a repressive effect of domestication and/or the lack of experience with live prey during a critical period in early life. Thus, as with sociability, inheritance (genes) and experience are compounding variables. Compared to wild cats, domestic varieties are less active and are generally more placid and have a lower reactivity toward sudden or novel stimuli, just as in domestic dogs.

Cats can become feral easily more than dogs; individual breeds of dog no longer have either the physique or behavior patterns to allow them to live independent of man. As with feral dogs, after a few generations feral cats may begin to breed to type and become very difficult to tame, even when raised from infancy.

There is less extreme variation in the cat in size, body proportions, and specific traits or specialist abilities than there is in the dog. Is it because the cat has not been domesticated for the same length of time as the dog? It may be that the mutability, or potential variability, within the domestic-cat gene pool is less than in the dog's. More likely, however, is the hypothesis that cats until recently were selectively bred for only two "specialist" abilities: to be both docile house pets and good mousers, keeping home, warehouse, or granary free of vermin. Selection for this latter ability would require essentially no change from its original wild form, either physically or psychologically. This would logically account for the small extent of species change over six thousand years of domestication; this is in contrast to the multidirectional selection in dog breeds and the resultant remarkable diversity of dogs today.

Only recently have standards been set for the different varieties of cats. Few are used for specific work (keeping down vermin). It will be interesting to see what new varieties may be developed as new mutants and recombinations of varieties over the next millennium. It will also be interesting to see, in the absence of any selection for specific traits or abilities, how future varieties of cat will differ in behavior and temperament. Coat color, in fact, may be an important guide and have considerable influence on the "linked" personality associated with it.

As in the dog, there are several unresolved behavioral problems which necessitate euthanasia if surgery or disciplinary training fails. Rigorous selective breeding will, it is hoped, eliminate or reduce their prevalence. Cats may also over time become more susceptible to emotional disorders, a dilemma greater today in dogs than in our more "inner-directed" and independent felines. Problems include: spraying, especially in males; the need to roam; motivation to hunt (and using owner as substitute prey); aggression towards own species and low sociability; clawing of furniture and drapes (possibly a social display); "hysteria" of some females in heat. Note, that, as in the dog, domestication has potentiated the sexuality of the cat. In *Understanding Your Cat*, these and other behavioral problems are discussed in detail.

Pet-Owner Bond

Wild animals that are relatively solitary as adults (most wild cats, raccoons, foxes, and other species) make good pets only rarely. As they mature, the close bond between owner—or parent in the natural state—is broken. In more gregarious species such as the wolf, this bond is maintained through a transformation at maturity: the parent (or owner) becomes the pack leader to the young adult. Thus, in dogs, the "parent-infant" relationship becomes a leader-follower relationship with the "master." In cats, the parent-infant relationship usually gives way to a "companion," or one-to-one, relationship with the owner. Quite often, however, the "parent-infant" relationship endures into adulthood, sometimes only partially. Cats will attempt to nurse and display other infantile behavior toward their owners—a phenomenon quite distinct from the care-soliciting actions of dependent "perpetual puppies."

It should be remembered that both domesticated cats and dogs become part of the household family in many ways. Some people see them merely as parasites, an aspect of immature human self-indulgence, or a source of disease and an introducer of filth into the home. For those with a more healthy outlook, the roles of the pet are many: playmate and confidant for children; child substitute or emotional "crutch"; companion; guard; status symbol; guide, for the blind; "cotherapist" for emotionally disturbed patients. The pet adapts and becomes closely attuned to the routines of the household, to the relationships between people and the other pets in the home. It learns the body language, moods, and habits of its owner—and may well be more closely attuned to its owner than the owner is to the pet!

It is not unusual for different species to become very close companions when raised together: parakeets and cats, rabbits and dogs. Cats and dogs may engage in reciprocal grooming and play; more than one cat has provided a much-needed source of companionship for a dog that must be left alone in the house for extended periods. Sexual imprinting may occur—as also between dog and owner—in a kitten or puppy raised with an adult dog or cat respectively. It is possible for some sexual activity to occur between cats

Some undesirable behaviors may be inherited, as are a number of physical defects, which, if not carefully selected against by breeders, can become quite common. Crossed eyes in the Siamese cat is one such abnormality which may severely limit the animal's visual capacities.

and dogs—but interbreeding will not result in offspring because the two species are genetically incompatible.

Nor is it unusual for a cat or dog to accept the other's offspring and allow it to nurse. Even virgin bitches will allow little kittens to attempt to nurse, and many lactating cats will readily accept a small orphan puppy. Maternal behavior in cats and dogs may have been influenced by domestication, but it is more likely that maternal hormones lead to an acceptance of many an alien species. One Irish setter, for example, regularly killed baby rabbits, and brought them home. But when she became pseudo-pregnant, she brought them home, attempted to nurse them, and was very protective toward them!

New "hybrid" dogs—"cockapoos" (cocker spaniel x poodle), "pulipoos" (puli x French poodle) and "shipoos" (shitzu x poodle) are becoming increasingly popular. Hybrid vigor—the best qualities of the parents being transmitted to the mixed offspring—may result in better quality pets than purebreds. Inbreeding and overbreeding are major causes of physical and psychological disorders, and have had disastrous consequences. The same holds true for the most popular variety of cats, the Siamese, which has more physical and behavioral problems than others.

Eugenics, Quality Control, and Reverence for Life

Some pets must be destroyed, if they are physically or psychologically abnormal. We must avoid unnecessary and unthinking destruction (which threatens many species) and uncontrolled animal propagation alike. This is the burden of our responsibility as stewards of the earth.

Humane destruction cannot be avoided. It must be perfected. We *must* kill to live, and kill selectively in order to maintain the quality of domestic and captive animals. This latter form of destruction is part of the evolutionary process of natural selection; to avoid it is to disrupt the process and to abdicate our responsibility.

A more humane alternative is sometimes found: for example, rather than destroy an animal, let it live but not breed, eliminating its potentially inheritable undesirable qualities from future generations. So-called eugenic practices to "improve the breed" for esthetic reasons—for example, trying to make all German pointers blond and blue-eyed—must be carefully evaluated on moral and ethical grounds. If we must be so selective, and in the process produce and propagate many animals that will be "wasted," let them live as nonbreeding pets.

We owe it both to ourselves and our animal kin to uphold the responsible ethic of reverence for all life. What we have done in the past and do today to domestic animals is not always humane or in their interest: we continue to use and exploit them, to alter them to adapt to new socio-environmental conditions and fulfill *our* needs. We must evaluate our needs and priorities against the needs and rights of others—be they people, cats, dogs, wolves, whales, pigs, or poultry. Ethical responsibility must become a part of man's global thought and action, and especially be expressed as an integral part of the utilitarian manipulation and exploitation of animals that we call domestication.

There is an increasing interest in owning wild animals as pets—the exotic foreign species and the more indigenous North American ones. Few if any work out as reliable, safe, and happy pets. Better options are those small animals that are relatively domesticated and have been loved for generations in captivity: rabbits, guinea pigs, cage birds, and aquarium fish. These interesting and adaptable pets will be given full consideration in the following chapters. Then we will return to the question of collecting and keeping wild animals as pets.

13

Some Words About Birds

I'LL NEVER FORGET my first veterinary encounter with a pet bird. An old lady came into the animal clinic with a cage containing her sick parakeet. At first glance, it was hard to pick out "Birdie" at all, since its cage was full of toys, perches, bells, balls, seed packs, cuttlebone, a ladder, a water bowl, two mirrors, and three plastic parakeets "for company." "Birdie's my only friend, and we live alone," the woman said. "You will—please—make her better?"

As it turned out, Birdie was simply eggbound (I'll explain what that means later) and her discomfort was easily remedied. What was more difficult was to grope through that avian playground in order to catch the bird and examine it. Such little birds will sometimes die of shock when they're handled, even gently, by a stranger. But we cured Birdie, and I still remember the old woman's gratitude.

Young and old have pet birds for many reasons—and the birds they pick may express their personalities as much as would the choice they'd make between a poodle or a Doberman. Some people who love the diminutive charm of the parakeet would find the macaw flashy. Some dote on the song of the canary; others enjoy the challenge of teaching a parrot or a parakeet to talk. But whatever the reasons, many people do choose a bird as a pet.

Because of decades of domestication, the parakeet is easiest to handle—especially for someone new to bird owning. Though particularly susceptible to drafts, parakeets are quite hardy. They thrive on human affection and can be trained to fly safely around the room—and sometimes even to talk.

The Indian myna is also a popular and entertaining pet because of its great vocal range and ability to mimic human speech. Similarly, parrots and cockatoos, which are good mimics and live for many years (as long as sixty to seventy), make excellent companions although they don't sing. Parrots are expensive, so beware of one with a cheap price tag, unless you are assured it is a common wild species; it may have been smuggled into the country or have been "unloaded" by someone because of its poor disposition.

Members of the parrot family are probably the most highly evolved of all birds. They are extremely intelligent, playful, and remarkably manipulative with their claws and beaks (they use their beaks for climbing as well as for cracking nuts). They don't need cages, preferring a jungle-gym arrangement of bars on which they can perch, climb, and swing (wings are clipped to prevent them from flying around). Some parrots do have bad dispositions, however; others tend to accept no one but specific members of their human family. And some become unpredictable with increasing age, and their beaks can inflict serious wounds.

Generally, though, birds are safe pets, with practically no diseases that they can transmit to man. In the past, imported parrots were unpopular because they carried "parrot disease" (or psittacosis), but today imported birds are rigorously quarantined to check this disease—and in the very rare cases it might occur, effective drugs are available to treat it.

Aside from their charm and personality, the main advantages to having caged birds as pets is that they require very little work each day to keep them healthy—and, generally speaking, their upkeep is inexpensive. No routine veterinary checkups, no shots.

Of course, you should start by getting a healthy *young* bird. Buy a bird as soon as it has its flight feathers (the breeder will point these out to you). This way, the bird will, early in its life, become acclimated to your presence in the same way a young puppy becomes socialized by its owner—making the pets easier to train and live with.

When buying, try to find a breeder in your area. You'll be surprised at the number of people who breed parakeets, canaries, pigeons, parrots, and so on. If you buy from a pet store, make sure you get a full health guarantee. Also obtain from the store (in writing) the promise of your money back or the substitution of another bird should your bird die ,or need veterinary treatment in the first two weeks after purchase. (Pet-shop owners are familiar with this code of ethics and should agree to your request readily.)

I advise against bird pets for very young children, who tend to grab at creatures (puppies and kittens, too) and can literally frighten a bird to death. On the other hand, a child with tender skin will probably react to a bird's love nip with pain and fear. For older children, from the age of six or so, however, a bird is a perfect pet—instilling in them a sense of responsibility, discipline, and affection. (All children should be taught, however, that birds do *not* like to be stroked. Birds are a species that, as a rule, does not like physical contact: they are also very sensitive to sudden movements and to loud noises, so any approach you or your children make to the bird should be slow and quiet.)

A Bird's Home

Essentially, all that is needed is a cage and stand, a perch, and a cloth cover to put over the cage at night so the bird will sleep. Rule number one: The cage should be too large rather than too small, so that your pet can stretch its wings. It should be set up in a spot free from drafts—tropi-

One of these could be your companion for life.   *(Debbie Bresler)*

cal birds chill easily and can die from a cold. Intense, bright sunlight can also be fatal to small birds, so try a spot where there will be only morning sun and no intense heat.

Ideally, the cage should have a removable sliding floor tray that can be lined with paper to collect the bird's droppings.

Keep your bird's home clean—especially its water container, which may develop a scum that could dause diarrhea and other ailments. Fresh water every day should be routine. And it is a wise precaution to clean and thoroughly dry the seed container and the perch every day, too. Also remove and refresh the bathing dish after your pet has had its dip.

Whether you go for an ornate antique cage or a simple modern one, make sure it's practical; it should be easy to clean, the seed and water hoppers accessible to both you and the bird, and the cage wires close enough together so the bird can't escape. Avoid painted or enameled cages; parakeets, especially, will nibble at the paint, and it's not good for them, even if it is nonpoisonous. And if, for some reason, you must repaint a cage, buy nontoxic enamel.

In large pet stores you will find a great variety of items you can put in the cage to make your bird feel at home. Both a fixed perch and a swinging perch are useful. A rough surface on the perch is an advantage because the bird can wipe its bill (the abrasion will also serve to keep its beak trimmed). A piece of cuttlebone in the cage is good for this purpose, too. Some birds enjoy ladders, bells, and hanging seed balls to peck at.

A parakeet will sometimes respond socially to an artificial companion, and may enjoy billing and cooing with a life-size plastic bird. This may sound a little bizarre, but remember that parakeets are highly gregarious and need company. Some young birds, like puppies, project this social need onto certain humans early in life, and treat their owners as "parents." Hand-raised ducks and starlings, for instance, will regard their owners as mothers and, even when they grow to adulthood, will follow their human parent, gaping and wing-flapping like a fledgling. In the same way, parakeets will bill and coo on an owner's shoulder, nibbling an earlobe or lock of hair for hours and twittering sweet nothings into a human ear. Part of this behavior is social and infantile, but some is sexual, and more than one parakeet owner has become the object of his pet's unrequited love.

A solitary caged bird may therefore suffer some confusion about sexual identity, as well as experience sexual frustration per se. The plastic companion bird can help in this regard by providing a social and sexual outlet for the bird's attentions. Another answer is a small mirror. This can be a potent stimulus: After being exposed to their own reflections, some male canaries and parakeets that have never sung before will suddenly start to sing.

However, you should be alert to problems that mirrors and plastic surrogates can sometimes cause. For instance, males may become so enamored and carried away with their own billing and cooing that their physical condition deteriorates. The bird may even regurgitate its food to share with its mirror image or plastic counterpart.

Similarly, a female may become overstimulated by these "creative" playthings and actually produce eggs (infertile ones, of course) or, worse, become constipated with eggs. This is what is meant by being eggbound, and if a bird is sluggish or sickly, your vet may discover that this is the reason. If these problems occur, it is advisable to remove the mirror or plastic bird for a while, if not permanently.

If you hope to breed a pair of birds, then obviously a larger cage will be needed. But be aware that not all birds will accept each other—conditions and the psychological mood have to be just right. Each species has its own requirements, which you will have to research if you plan to go on to breeding. Usually, a nesting box or plastic nest cup and nesting material (hay, shredded paper, and so on) may help trigger breeding in all species except the parakeet, which does not particularly need such nesting material. Expect your birds to molt and pull out their feathers in order to line the nest, and many species develop a bare, swollen brood patch on their breasts as a result. Some people confuse this with a skin disease and apply medication, but it is quite normal during the incubation period.

A Bird's Food

Most birds need the same diet, with slight differences in the balance of ingredients. There are commercial products tailored for each type of bird, and they are generally quite good. These bird foods, which are a mixture of seeds and vitamins, can be supplemented with small quantities of fruits and fresh greens, such as spinach, dandelion, and carrot. Individual birds vary in their preference for fruit, and pollies do indeed like crackers (plain or unsalted— they're good for parrots).

Nutritional deficiencies can, of course, cause problems. Many people write to me about their parakeets' beaks becoming "soft." This is due to a lack of vitamins and essential minerals, and I advise adding a few drops of cod-liver oil to the bird's diet, as well as a sprinkling of bone flour, bone meal, or calcium lactate (especially if it will not eat cuttlebone shell). These may be purchased at any pet store.

Another frequent symptom of a nutritional lack is a long or excessive molting. If such a condition exists, make very sure that your bird's diet is mixed and varied—that it includes seeds, fruits, and vegetables. Cuttle, fish bone and some grit are also needed to help the bird digest seeds. And of course sunlight (no direct rays, but diffuse ultraviolet light) is vital to the bird's health.

A Bird's Care

Routinely, your bird's beak and claws should be clipped. Overgrown nails prevent a bird from grasping his perch correctly and may catch on bars or papers and be torn out accidentally. Though owners often back off from manicuring, it's really quite simple. If you hold the bird gently and put its leg up to the light, you will clearly see where the nail ends and tissue begins. So use a small nipper or nail clippers, and snip carefully.

To trim the beak, again hold the bird up to a strong light so that you can see the dark blood vessels: then, with strong, straight manicure nippers, remove the chalky excess growth, cutting back to the horny live tissue, following the natural line of the beak.

Cuttlebone should provide the minerals to keep a bird's beak strong; together with seeds that the bird must dehusk, it will help control further growth of the beak horn. Excessive growth and deformity of the beak may be due to mites; veterinary advice must then be sought.

If your bird's feathers are broken and in poor condition, a number of factors may be involved—ranging from nutritional deficiency to lice to "French molt," a complex condition in which the normal regeneration and growth of the feathers is disrupted. If you suspect any of these things, you may need a vet's advice.

Provide a bath bowl, but then allow the bird to follow its own pattern for bathing—and don't worry about it.

At the base of the tail, birds have a preening gland; its secretion is used to anoint their feathers and keep them in good condition. A healthy bird will look sleek and shiny because it preens itself regularly; a sick bird will have an unkempt appearance because it has stopped preening itself. You can also recognize sickness in your pet if its feathers are ruffled (in order to keep warm), if its droppings are runny or bloody, or if it's not eating.

A Bird's Special Problems

Certainly, one of a bird's special bugaboos is a cat. In most cases, a cat in the home will terrorize a bird—so letting your pet out of its cage to fly around the room is *verbot-*

en. If raised together, however, cat and bird—just like cat and dog or dog and bird—can become socialized and grow up to coexist. In fact, remarkable and enduring companionships have been reported. If you already have a cat in the house, though, it's very risky to bring in a bird; cats are clever and persistent when it comes to catching prey, even one in a cage several feet off the ground.

A problem of a different sort is that it is difficult to tell the sex of birds because their external genitals are almost identical. If the sex of your bird matters to you, you'll have to check other signs, such as the color of its plumage—and, with parakeets, a purple cere or horny growth on the bills of the male bird (the female's cere is brownish). Another sign is that only male birds sing. (If injected with male hormones early in life, however, female birds may later sing.)

When a singing bird, such as a canary or parakeet, stops warbling, the owner usually goes into mini-shock. Often this silence is merely because the bird is going through a quiet phase in his reproductive cycle and needs to be re-stimulated, come springtime, by a companion. If spring doesn't set him caroling, then I advise trying a mirror, a plastic companion, or a female bird for company.

A Bird's Training

If your bird doesn't sing, it may be trained to speak or, more accurately, to mimic speech. Parakeets and parrots are most noted for this ability. A bird must be taught when it's very young. There are numerous ways to do this, from reward training (with food) to simple repetition. There are also records you can buy, or you can make tape recordings of your own voice. If you have a bird with this speech potential, check your library shelves for suggestions.

It's also worth releasing your bird in a room of your home from time to time so it can enjoy more freedom. Again, a training phase for flight is necessary, and it's best done from very early birdhood on. And before you start, make certain that the room is safe—and that means no fires (lighted candles or embers in the fireplace), no open chimneys or windows, no unguarded electric fans, no other animals.

For any kind of training to be effective, you must start with a happy bird that feels loved. How do you show affection to a bird? Mimic the bird's billing and cooing movements. Talk to it gently. Whistle to it. Sing to it. But do *not* stroke or pet it unless it clearly enjoys your touch.

Can birds, like dogs and cats, become neurotic? It is true they sometimes display erratic behavior, which human beings often interpret as neurotic. For instance, one man had a male parakeet who refused to breed with the female. When the female died, the owner put another male into the cage for companionship. Suddenly, the first bird started to display female sexual behavior. "Is my bird a homosexual?" asked the owner. No—the signals for sex and submission are similar. Male number one was simply showing submission to male number two—probably out of a sudden insecurity.

Not long ago I was on a research project in the jungles of southern India. There I saw a profusion of long-tailed green- and rose-headed parakeets and myriads of tiny finches flitting and chattering by the river. In many parts of the world these birds are caught—as are countless other finches, mynas, and parrots in countries all over Asia, the Far East, and South America. They are packed tightly into flimsy crates and exported to Europe and America for sale in pet stores. Few will ever reach their destination, dying of shock, overcrowding, and thirst on the way. So if you plan to enjoy a cage bird as a pet, be sure that you don't buy a rare wild one that's been imported; if the bird is a rare or endangered species, you may be supporting an inhumane and ecologically disruptive practice. Purchase a bird from a breeder or a trustworthy pet store only if the owner assures you that the birds are neither imported nor native American species that have been caught in the wild.

Cage birds make beautiful pets. And to those who may

not like the idea of any creature being restrained in a cage, the fact is that a well-adapted bird sees its cage as its territory and refuge, and will be responsive and happy if you give it what all creatures thrive on—sensible care as well as affection.

14

Parakeets and Budgerigars

IF YOU ARE thinking of buying a cage bird, be sure it was hatched and raised in captivity. And if you already have a parakeet, read on and check out if you are doing all that you should for your pet. I do get a lot of questions from owners about their cage birds, and although we don't have all the answers about them yet, a good deal *is* known and every cage-bird owner should have such knowledge for the well-being of their companions.

I believe that such knowledge can also help us understand and therefore appreciate and even communicate better with our pets.

The original parakeets or budgerigars, often called "budgies" today, were called "betcherrygahs" by the Aborigines of Australia, where they live in large, noisy flocks. They were first bred in captivity in England. Their natural "wild" color is green with black and yellow markings. Through selective breeding over the past 130 years or so, a great variety of color types, shades, and combinations have been created: blue, white and green, yellow, mauve, violet, cinnamon, grey, cobalt—and on and on! Green being the dominant color in "budgies" in the wild, if a rare blue or yellow mutant were to be hatched, its offspring would be green, since it would most probably mate with a green bird. In captivity, though, such natural color mutants can be selected out and bred to similar mutants, thus a wide range of color types can be developed.

Parakeets, being naturally gregarious, thrive in a walk-in aviary or flight shed, large enough to house many birds. They adapt well to mild outdoor climates, but the open flight cage should include a warm shed with nest boxes and perches attached. The flight cage, ideally, should be covered by a double layer of one half- or one fourth-inch wire mesh as a cat deterrent. A double door into the shed is essential to prevent the birds from accidentally escaping.

There are many varieties of indoor cage to house one or two birds. The birds like cages that include some horizontal bars upon which they can climb up and down the sides. If all the cage bars are vertical, a ladder or suitable climbing "jungle gym" will be appreciated by any bird. And the bigger the cage the better.

Parakeets live anywhere from eight to fifteen years. Some authorities believe those birds that have been forced to mature quickly for show purposes are soft and will not live as long.

Be sure the parakeet is young when you buy it—ideally less than eight weeks out of the nest. An older bird is harder to train since it is less likely to become attached or "imprinted" to its owners. Young birds, especially the ones with darker wings, have barring on the forehead: these marks recede by the time the birds are three months old. If you don't see these marks in a darker-colored bird, you know that it is past the optimal age for imprinting. Young birds of all colors have black eyes; after they molt into adult plumage at three months of age, the iris—the ring around the pupil—turns white. After the molt, there's no way of telling the bird's age. If it has spent the crucial formative period with other birds, it won't become an attached and talkative companion. Males, though, are less "nippy" than females and easier to train for a beginner.

Unlike many species of birds in which only the male

sings, it doesn't matter with parakeets: both sexes are chat-
terers. They aren't solitary singers. The more sociable they
feel with you, the more they will chatter; therefore, the
more sociable the birds are, the more "accessible" their
vocal behavior will be in your efforts to teach them to talk.

When you first get your bird, don't begin right off trying
to teach it to talk. Give it a few days to settle down and lose
its fear of you. Talk gently, move slowly, and after three or
four days offer it a little food on your fingertip—a spring of
millet is a good lure. Repeating this will allow it to become
accustomed to you and teach it to trust. Don't grab the bird,
but allow it to explore your hand, taste and nip the skin, and
perch on your finger. While talking to your bird try gently
scratching the back or side of his head. A tilted head, as
though asking for more, will let you know you are getting
through to him! After a couple of weeks, let it out of the
cage to fly about in the room. They love to exercise and explore. A caged bird may otherwise become obese, bored,
and may develop vices and neurotic actions. Block off all
chimneys, screen any open fires, and keep other household
pets away—especially cats! Draw the curtains: birds don't
understand that clear glass is solid and can injure themselves trying to fly through a window or glass screen door.

Many budgies enjoy baths, either in a bowl of water (in
or out of the cage) or under a faucet gently running with
lukewarm water. Because of the oil on their feathers, they
soon dry off.

Once your parakeet is settled in, you can start teaching it
to talk. Like their cousins, the parrots, they are accurate little mimics. Keep repeating the same word—a tape recorder
near the cage, repeating the word over and over, will help
while you are out; eventually your bird will attempt to imi-
tate the word in its own squeaky little voice. "Hello (whatever his name is)" is good for a start. The imitation will improve with practice. However, it is all but impossible to
teach a parakeet to talk if it can hear other parakeets. One
parakeet in a cage may talk, but two will rarely do so.

So one of your earliest decisions may be made uncon-

sciously and greatly influence both socialization and a
bird's talking. You may want to have a talking bird; but the
bird's need for a companion bird may become evident. If
you have one bird and imprint it on you, it may not take
well to a mate introduced later in life. And if they do pair
up, it may stop talking to you from then on!

One theory behind training a parakeet to talk is that it
comes to regard the word you keep saying as your call. Always say it with the same pitch and intonation. After a couple of weeks of saying the same word, make the bird feel a
little lonely: give your "call" from another room. As soon
as the bird responds, go at once to it and lavish it with attention. This will encourage it to learn other calls (words). For
a bird that won't talk much, try removing its toys for a
while—they may be distracting it from its lessons, prevent-
ing it from being more dependent upon you!

Life alone in a cage may seem cruel, especially considering parakeets' natural gregariousness; domestication has
affected this trait little if at all. They love company. If you
house just one talker in a cage, you must be sure to provide
suitable substitutes to compensate for the lack of social
contacts.

The first substitute is you—your hand is particularly
significant. It's a perch, a source of food, and, for some
birds, it is a companion to bill and coo with. Don't be
alarmed if your bird starts to nibble on a fingernail. It re-
sembles the bill of another bird; your parakeet is engaging
in a social act of touching, tasting, and grooming.

Parakeet mates bill and coo together for hours in this
manner. Such behavior in adults may be derived from the
billing and cooing of parents with their fledgling babies
while feeding them. (They also produce a kind of milk from
the crop, or throat stomach, for their offspring.) Other species of bird, like the tern and roadrunner, not only bill and
coo as adults, but actually feed their mates with a "token"
morsel of fish or lizard, and the mate "regresses" and behaves like an infant in this elaborate courtship ritual. Your
parakeet won't feed you in this way, but the sociable billing

and cooing directed toward your fingers may be derived from infant feeding. And don't be surprised if your parakeet sometimes becomes a little sexually aroused while engaged in such play. After all, you are a bird-companion substitute!

Your head and face are another source of substitute social interaction. Many birds enjoy climbing across your shoulder, nibbling your earlobes, even climbing up your head by grasping your hair. Some birds will nibble-preen hair. Some enjoy kissing, too—gently billing and cooing on your lips when you coo to the bird perched on your shoulder.

Life in the cage should be enriched to make residence interesting. Parakeets are curious, manipulative, and intelligent little birds.

Ladders, ropes to climb or used to ring a bell, a seed bell, a swinging perch, a ball, a plastic companion parakeet, even a mirror to provide a reflection at which to bill and coo, are all useful cage accessories. A solid perch should be fixed near the food and water dispensers. Perches should be no less than one half-inch in diameter, as trying to grip a very narrow perch can cause the bird considerable pain.

Feeding your parakeet is no problem. A wide variety of commercial preparations is available. A mixture of plain canary seeds mixed with various kinds of millet and sunflower seeds forms the basic diet. Parakeets dehusk the seeds stripping off the outer seed shell and eating the inner kernel. If the seed bowl fills with husks, remove the husks daily (or as frequently as required) and add fresh seed. All small creatures have high metabolic rates and, because of small stomach capacities, have to eat more or less constantly during waking hours.

Parakeets, like all seed- and grain-eating birds, have a gizzard—a muscular stomach that grinds up the food they eat. The grinding process is aided by small amounts of ingested gravel stored in the gizzard. If no gravel is provided, they will not be able to digest their food; food would pass through undigested and intestinal problems might develop. So always provide your bird with a little fine gravel.

A spray of millet seed hung in the cage is a good idea. But not too much too often—it's fattening! A piece of cuttlefish bone or an iodized mineral block is essential; they provide growing birds with plenty of calcium. Calcium is essential for renewed feather growth, for maintaining the nails and beak, and for proper eggshell development if your bird is to be bred.

Some parakeet owners never feed their birds any greens. Yet the birds seem to thrive anyway. But greens provide essential minerals, vitamins, and other nutrients; try a little *well-washed* spinach, lettuce, and dandelions. If your bird doesn't develop any intestinal upsets and enjoys the greens, by all means provide them. Another "natural food" supplement is a bunch of wild (or lawn) grasses that have just gone to seed; tie a bunch inside the cage. But always remember—wash the grass thoroughly first to remove any insecticides, herbicide residues, and possible contaminants from diseased wild birds. Some budgies relish an occasional slice of carrot or apple, or a teaspoon full of regular seed that has been allowed to sprout in a little cold water for a few days.

Fresh water should be given daily. A gravity water bottle with an inverted dropper spout easily and conveniently dispenses the small amount they require.

Clean the seed and water containers every few days. Scrub out the cage every week with a mild disinfectant. Then add a fresh cage-floor liner of paper sprinkled with sand, or a commercial litter paper liner. Cleanliness reduces the chances of sickness.

A bird that is kept clean, dry, well fed, and warm is not likely to get sick. But a few pointers are important to note.

Any sudden change in its behavior—won't eat, won't talk, isn't playful and just sits on its perch with its feathers fluffed out—may mean some form of illness. Excessively runny droppings could mean a mild intestinal upset. Withdraw all greens and gravel for a day; if things aren't any better within twenty-four hours, call your vet. On the other hand, constipation sometimes occurs in birds of all ages.

Parakeets are not just dumb birds. They are highly sociable, intelligent, and affectionate. *(Mike Johnson, HSUS)*

Providing a little green foodstuffs helps in most cases and mixing a little cod-liver oil (or Vitamin A and D drops) with the seed.

Parakeets are prone to respiratory infections—sneezing and a slight nasal or eye discharge could indicate pneumonia.

As parakeets get older, they tend to develop tumors. Sometimes these are simply benign fatty growths (lipomas). If the growth interferes with the bird's movements or is becoming infected, it may be removed surgically by your veterinarian. While great advances have been made in veterinary anesthesia and surgery, not all vets are equipped to handle such tiny patients. Because of their extremely sensitive nervous systems, parakeets are prone to die of shock and so are risky patients to treat. Sometimes, though, it's worth taking the risk.

A not uncommon ailment is egg-binding or impaction. Some bird authorities advise massaging the hind end with warm olive oil to relax the muscles of the cloaca. The offending egg may be passed as a result.

Particularly common are overgrown, sometimes deformed, beaks and overlong nails. A gritty surface on the perch may help prevent this. But once such growths have occurred, one must trim them with a good pair of nail clippers. Once you have been shown by a knowledgeable friend or vet, you will know to cut below the pink "quick" of the nail and so avoid bleeding. The beak should be trimmed back to the normal length. Be careful not to snip the bird's tongue! Excessive beak growth and scales at the base—and also on the legs—may indicate a mite infestation. Your veterinarian can prescribe a suitable ointment.

The so-called French molt is a common problem, perhaps due to a combination of nutritional and hereditary factors. In this situation, tail and wing feathers fall out, leaving the bird sadly bedraggled. There is no reliable known cure. Such birds should not be used for breeding. Perpetual molting may be caused by erratic fluctuations in room temperature. Keeping the bird in a stable, mild environment and providing it with vitamin supplements may help.

Sometimes it's not French molt—the bird may simply be a feather plucker. It may pull out its own feathers and/or those of a companion. This "vice," which may either be inherited or come as a consequence of boredom, is hard to inhibit. Offending birds are best caged alone; provide plenty of playthings to keep them busy and otherwise distracted!

All birds molt once a year. The process can take up to three months, during part of which they may appear listless. A good diet is essential during this period to aid feather regeneration.

Food regurgitation could mean an impacted or infected crop (the "first stomach," located in the throat, of the budgie). Sometimes, though, in males, it is a normal part of courtship behavior. But if he's doing it on his mirror or plastic companion budgie, remove such toys or he will soon lose condition!

Many bird owners cover the cage at night with an opaque drape. Like hooding a falcon, covering the cage quickly switches the bird off and it will go right to sleep. This is not essential; turning the lights off will suffice. Recent research has shown that the pineal gland, the so-called third eye found in the brains of birds, is very sensitive to daily and seasonal changes in daylight length and intensity and acts as a governor, regulating the bird's activity cycles.

This is why I believe indoor birds should be close to a window (but *not* in direct sunlight), so they then can be "in tune" with the natural rhythms of the seasons. This will help insure normal molting and other natural cyclic physiological and behavioral activities, easily disrupted if it is placed in a room where it will receive mainly artificial light at irregular, human-patterned intervals.

Parakeets breed readily in captivity. Pairing is best undertaken in March or April. Both birds should be in top physical condition; otherwise infertile eggs may result, or, with an inadequately nourished mother, the chick embryos may not develop or hatch. A dull or pale cere (the colored ridge at the base of the beak) may mean poor condition: it should be shiny blue in the male and dark brown or creamy-pink in the female. Young birds of either sex have dull blue ceres; males have rather bigger, "bolder" heads and a slightly purple tinge to the cere.

Within hours, a newly introduced pair should settle down. If scuffles continue, the birds will have to be separated; "arranged" marriages don't always work! A pair is more likely to breed if the male can hear the calls of a second male; this seems to stimulate sperm production.

Parakeets nest in tree hollows in the wild, and don't make a nest inside the tree. All they need to simulate a nest is a small box placed on the floor of the cage, provided with many small ventilation holes, and one two-inch entry hole; inside the box, a shallow scooped-out cup, say five inches across and one-half inch deep. Four to seven eggs may be laid, one each day. The chicks will hatch after seventeen to eighteen days of incubation. Father feeds the mother while she is sitting on the eggs, and will help feed the featherless chicks. The chicks mature rapidly and leave the nest box after four to five weeks. They may be put in a separate cage once they are able to fend effectively for themselves.

For families in apartments, elderly people, for others who want a pet easy to care for and fun as a companion, the parakeet is a certain success.

15

Do's and Don'ts About Tropical (Aquarium) Fish*

FISH SEEM TO be somewhere between the worlds of potted plants and pet animals: they don't need exercise, and you can't exactly play or talk with them.

A nicely arranged aquarium illuminated and filled with brightly colored tropical fish is certainly an attractive decoration for home or apartment. And once everything is set in balance and running smoothly, a minimum of routine attention is required.

I think one reason many people don't have an aquarium is that they think it would be too much of a chore, or requires much knowledge to keep such delicate creatures alive. This is far from the truth. There is a set of rules anyone can follow to insure the easy establishment of a home aquarium and its wholly successful maintenance. There's no need to be intimidated!

Another deterrent commonly cited is the initial cost. You don't have to begin with a fifty-gallon tank: a fifteen-gallon tank, not at all expensive, will suffice to get you started. Later you may wish to graduate to bigger and better aquariums.

I suspect that a major reason many people don't fancy keeping a tropical aquarium is that they simply don't see

*Fresh-water fish as distinct from salt-water species.

anything in keeping fish. I agree that it's hardly right to keep pets for decoration alone (and heaven forbid, but many purebred dogs do seem to be kept around as nothing more than decorator items!).

A well-stocked, healthy aquarium, however, is more than just another piece of household decor. When you know what's going on inside the tank, you have a glimpse into another world: a fascinating and enthralling micro-universe of life utterly different from ours. Many tropical-fish owners soon learn to recognize the different temperaments and moods of their fish, and the various intra- and inter-species relationships between them. Observing one's fish is wholly absorbing and at the same time relaxing. There are important lessons to learn about life, death, reproduction, and the balance of life in the aquarium. A fish tank in a classroom exposes different age groups to a whole range of study, from behavior, ecology, and evolution to pollution and conservation.

Keeping tropical fish for pure enjoyment seems to be an ancient practice. The Chinese nobility, who kept goldfish in carved stone basins some thousand years ago, are thought to be the first aquarium keepers. But at the King Tut exhibit I recently saw a mosaic inlay depicting a room scene from ancient Egypt, against one wall of which was shown what seemed to be a large glass aquarium containing two or three fish!

Conservation note: a very high price tag on a fish could mean that it's rare, hard to breed in captivity, or was caught in the wild. *Never* buy a tropical fish that wasn't bred in captivity.

Basic Requirements

Plastic aquariums are cheap and leakproof but are easily scratched. The more you pay, the better tank you will get: a glass tank with a stainless steel frame is the most durable. Water must be maintained at a constant seventy-five de-

Many tropical fish have fascinating behavior patterns. Here, two gourami are "kissing"—a ritual display of aggression.

grees. A reliable heater, with a thermostatic control to keep the correct temperature and a thermometer, is an inexpensive but essential item.

A cover is also required, primarily to prevent fish from accidentally leaping out. It also prevents dust from dirtying the water and reduces the rate of water loss through evaporation. The cover should be of a design allowing fresh air to circulate over the water surface. Oxygen dissolves from the air through the surface of the water: the greater the surface area, the more oxygen will permeate the water.

Fish can't drown, but they will suffocate if the water's oxygen supply is inadequate. For this reason, avoid the temptation of overcrowding your tank. Fifteen one-and-a-half to two-inch fish in a fifteen-gallon tank is about the right population. You may wish to buy a mechanical air pump. This isn't a filter or water cleaner. It simply adds more oxygen to the water.

Plants, too, remove carbon dioxide from the water and add oxygen as a waste product of photosynthesis. A light source is essential for the plants to produce oxygen. An artificial lighting strip built into a light reflector set in the aquarium cover is the most reliable. This can be set on a twelve-hour on/off cycle with a timer switch. Gro-lux warm white fluorescent lighting is popular, a twenty-watt lamp being adequate for a two-foot tank. Avoid placing the tank near a window. Direct sunlight may overheat the water and too much light can lead to discolored water, due to over-growth of algae, and sickly fish and plants.

Setting Up

The floor of the aquarium should be layered with well-washed aquarium grit or gravel—about twenty-five pounds for a two-foot aquarium. Add decorative rocks and a few clumps of freshwater plants secured so they will soon take root in the gravel. Cover all this with newspaper to keep the gravel from churning up and slowly pour in cold fresh water until the level is about three inches below the top of the tank. Then remove the newspaper, and finally, with the light cycle and the aerator, if you have one, working, let the tank settle for a week before you introduce any fish. This step is essential for the removal of any chemicals in the water. If the water in your area is very hard, boil and cool it first, then use only the top half of the kettle.

You may want to purchase a water filter to keep the tank free of debris. A manually operated suction tube will do just as well for a small tank, however. A water filter is prob-

ably a better buy for most aquariums than an aerator, provided your fish tank isn't overstocked. Top up the tank
each week with "aged" water (left standing for twenty-four
hours) to replenish water lost through evaporation. A "balanced" tank needs cleaning out only every four to six
months. Change the activated charcoal in the filter every
six weeks or so. Wash out the spun glass or other filter element as needed.

Adding Life

A wide variety of attractive water plants is available at
low cost: hygrophila from Asia, the Amazon sword plant,
echinodorus and cabombas from South America, the Indian
or water fern, leafy ludwigias, and fast-growing elodea or
Canadian weed. Vallisneria or eel grass is very decorative;
and hornwort and myriophyllum are good oxygen produc-
ers. Don't buy plastic plants—they provide no oxygen and
may even be toxic to aquarium life.

One form of life that inevitably turns up in the tank is
some form of algae. Algae are microscopic plants that appear as a green or brownish film growing on the inside of
the tank. They may also coat the larger plants and spread to
make the water murky and smelly. This can be due to *eu-
trophication*—the environment in the tank becoming too
rich. You may be overfeeding your fish or giving too much
artificial light. Try cutting down both for a couple of weeks
and see if this helps clear the water.

You can buy chemicals designed to kill algae, but it's best
not to resort to such unnatural warfare.

A rubber scraper or razor blade can be used to scrape the
tank sides clean. Some people like to add three or four
ramshorn snails to help keep the tank clean. It is debatable
just how much effect they have, but they are at least interesting additions to the aquarium.

Before you go to purchase your selection of fish, be sure
your aquarium is all set up and ready for them.

Every aquarium should have at least one natural "vacuum cleaner." The different types commonly available all belong to the catfish family. They help keep the sides and bottom of the tank clean.

If the pet-store salesperson can't advise you on which fish to buy and which species get along together best, find someone in another store who can. Some species of fish, like the cichlids, can be truculent bullies and may claim the entire aquarium as their territory. Avoid trouble by becoming an educated consumer.

Most of the varieties of fish offered for sale are very sociable. You should buy at least a pair of each species since they like to swim and live close together. A pair of fairly large "kissing" gouramis or angelfish makes a good nucleus for the population. If some are too large, the larger species may bully the smaller. This can be avoided by providing plenty of vegetation cover in which the smaller fish may seek shelter, and by *never* overcrowding the tank with fish. Other species prefer to live in shoals of six or more; unless you have a very large tank, stick to the smaller varieties.

Various species of tetra are peaceable additions to a tank, as are the communal barbs and zebra fish. Every tank should include some live-bearing fish; these species don't lay eggs but give birth to live fry. Types include the swordtails, guppies, platys, and mollies. Five or six of these in the tank will stay together as a small shoal and add considerably to the diversity of form and behavior in the tank. The adults eat many of the young; the hardiest survive into adulthood.

Waste no time in getting your new fish home—a chill can kill. Avoid temperature shock by placing them still in their water-filled containers directly into the aquarium. After a couple of hours cut the bags and let them out. Be sure to quarantine any new additions to an established tank for a few days in a "hospital" aquarium, or if this is not available, in a covered glass beaker wired to the inside of your aquarium. Always have a net handy to catch any sick fish: never try to catch them with your hands.

Never overcrowd your aquarium like this one!

A well-balanced aquarium is a miniature universe which is both decorative and entertaining.

Once you become tuned in to your aquarium residents, you will discover what different characters lie behind those unblinking fish eyes. They have clear likes and dislikes, social rivalries, and a pecking or dominance order, and very often establish territorial regions in certain parts of the tank. An aquarium watcher also learns how fish communicate: watching as they position their bodies up, down, or sideways, raising or lowering their fins in threat or submission. Some even change color with emotion and may develop bright colors during the breeding season.

A rubber feeding ring attached to the side of the tank will keep the dry food flakes in one place on the surface of the water, and prevents wastage. Buy a variety of dry fish foods, but don't overlook giving your fish natural fresh foods occasionally. Never overfeed: just add a few morsels of shredded raw meat, earthworm, lettuce, small woodlice, or—best of all, if you can find them—a few daphnia (water fleas) or tubifex worms.

There are a number of fish diseases for which you should be on the lookout. Ich, or white spot disease, is caused by a parasite that feeds on the blood and skin of the host. It must be treated promptly or it may spread and you may lose all your fish. It often occurs when a new fish is introduced into a tank of healthy ones and proves to be infected. First, raise the temperature of the tank five to seven degrees. Then add a few drops of five percent methylene blue—just enough to tinge the water blue. Add a few drops each day for a week.

Fungus diseases, causing fin rot and cotton-wool-like growths on the body, are quite common. You can try home medication: gently swab each diseased fish with a strong salt solution before placing it in a separate "hospital" tank containing two ounces of rock salt to each gallon of water. Keep the fish in the "hospital" for four or five days, during which time it should have recovered. You can purchase prepared fungicides from your pet store. A new drug, Furanace (from Abbot Labs), is quite effective against a number of tropical fish diseases and should be available in your pet store now.

Fish gulping at the surface indicates that the tank water is low in oxygen. A broken, choked, or disconnected pump or filter may be to blame, if the tank isn't simply overcrowded or polluted.

I hope that these tips will help you keep your aquarium and fish bright and healthy. There are few things more beautiful and fascinating than the miniature universe of a tropical fish aquarium. More than just an attractive addition to the decor, an aquarium provides a source of esthetic pleasure and relaxation and constant learning experiences in both home and classroom—for children of all ages.

16

Hamsters and Gerbils

I MET MY first hamsters at a local Home and Garden Show in England. They were on exhibit on a table, between rows of garden flower arrangements, homemade cakes and preserves and cages of rabbits and parakeets. I recall my surprise and excitement. Never before had I seen such blackberry-eyed, stump-tail balls of cuddly brown fur.

I was twelve years old at the time and the exhibitor, a Mr. Hobson, told me how rare hamsters were. The animals originated in Syria and if I was really interested in them, I should visit his "hamstery" and learn more about them before I purchased one. A few weeks later I had two, a male and female (naturally), and was a member of the North and Midlands Hamster Club. Hamster owners formed little social worlds too; at the shows, hamsters were judged against standards for the two colors then existing—gold and agouti. Albinos, piebalds, creams, tortoiseshells, and other color types were unknown then. And recently a long-haired woolly type has been developed!

Had gerbils been around then too, I'm sure my avid interest in attractive and entertaining pets would have embraced them as well! Gerbils, however, came onto the pet scene in England several years after the golden or Syrian hamster.

Today both species are readily available in pet stores (at about two to four dollars apiece) and have also become an integral part of the animal research colonies of many universities and laboratories. They may be the ideal pets for young children old enough to be responsible for their care. Since they thrive in small cages or aquariums—(and if their spaces are kept clean, don't smell at all)— they are excellent apartment pets. No child need be deprived of the benefits of keeping a pet; or, as I would rather redefine it, the benefit of being the guardian and caretaker (not owner or master) of such companion (not "pet") animals. And the hamsters of my youth were hardly "pets" anyway: most of them still had pretty wild temperaments and often bit the hand that fed or petted it!

Hamsters, and gerbils especially, have been bred for tractable temperaments. They are now popular in kindergarten and grade school classrooms. Some children's hospitals even employ them as "cotherapists"; the little animals provide invalid and emotionally disturbed children with entertainment, enjoyment, and distraction, and, most importantly, a real link with life.

Because they do have different qualities and requirements, I will discuss the general care and characteristics of hamsters and gerbils separately, beginning, of course, as I did, with hamsters. The name is derived from the German word *hamstern*, which means to hoard. This is the most characteristic quality of the hamster. It stuffs food into its cheek pouches to carry home and quickly builds up a store or granary of goodies in some part of its nest.

There are various species of hamster. The wild European one is still considered a threat to agriculture in some areas. Most of the hamsters available in pet stores are descendants of a family found in northern Syria and successfully propagated at Hebrew University in Jerusalem.

When fully grown, a hamster is six to seven inches long and weighs about four ounces. Females are slightly larger than males and are usually more aggressive. Hamsters are best kept in separate cages, not only to control breeding, but also to prevent fighting. Males have a "boom" or more oval posterior due to the presence of testicles. One can, therefore, easily sex them.

Hamsters have stumpy little tails. They usually sport a dark stripe across each cheek and a charcoal gray waistcoat, or vest mark, on their chests, set off by cream-colored under-fur. This waistcoat serves a special function in social behavior. When hamsters engage in a fight, they rear up on their hind legs, chatter their teeth, and display this chest vest. Hamsters with large vests (experimentally made larger by applying a little dye) usually turn out to be winners.

These endearing creatures are nocturnal, preferring in the wild to sleep during the day, becoming active in the early evening. With domestication and habituation to the daytime activities in the home, they change from their natural rhythm apparently without undue stress.

The average life span of a hamster is from two to three years. It is best to buy one that is four to eight weeks old, since this is the best age to tame them. Get your hamster used to being handled while it's still young. A poorly socialized hamster is likely to be more fearful and will probably bite. (This also holds true for gerbils; they are, however, basically more docile, less likely to bite, than hamsters.)

I recommend that when you first buy one of these young rodents, you sit down with it on the floor or on a sofa. Scoop it up gently in both hands. Be sure there is a soft surface beneath the animal in case it falls or escapes from your hands. If you are sitting down, it will of course have less of a fall. Let the new pet explore around you: it must be allowed time to get used to your odor. Talk to it gently as well. Avoid sudden movements and noises; both hamsters and gerbils are easily frightened. Don't allow it to run around the house—(even if you don't have a cat or dog that could kill it). I learned this the hard way. The little animals can be easily trodden upon accidentally, be caught or crushed by a door, or lost for days—or forever, if they crawl under the floorboards or behind the wall via a radiator pipe hole or other opening.

The hamster—a cuddly and interesting pet.

Cages

Both hamsters and gerbils should be secured in chew-proof cages: with their teeth and their persistent natures they soon will be running free if their enclosure is made of wood. Cages should have solid sides—and no bars; hamsters and gerbils like to dig and burrow and will kick out bedding and litter between the bars all over the place! Metal cages and aquarium tanks are ideal.

Cages should be lined with a floor litter of sawdust or wood shavings (or sand for gerbils). Provide some form of bedding material—hay or newspaper—out of which they can make a nest. Some sort of crawlspace—tin can, or plant pot on its side—makes an attractive quiet corner for the pet. Ladders, exercise wheels, and toys may be added to make the cage a more complex and stimulating environment. The enclosure should be in a warm, draught-free place and should never be in direct sunlight.

All the dirty floor litter should be taken up every week. The cage and all its contents should be scrubbed thoroughly and cleaned every two or three weeks, and fresh bedding and litter placed in the cage. Many hamsters and gerbils use just one corner of their enclosure as a toilet; this makes cleaning up very easy. A litter tray is useful for cleaning up, and a flat paint scraper may also come in handy as a scoop. Because they are desert animals and pass less urine, gerbils require even less regular cleaning out than hamsters. If your hamster likes to store large quantities of food, clean out the store every couple of days; it is likely to turn moldy or rancid, causing the cage to smell, perhaps sickening your hamster.

A safe container should be on hand in which to put the pet while its cage is being cleaned and dried. Don't let gerbils or hamsters wander freely on a table top or the kitchen sink area. They are nearsighted and may fall and injure themselves.

Like many rodents, gerbils and hamsters eat their own feces. In this way they obtain essential B vitamins. Over-zealous cage cleaning therefore should be avoided!

Food and Water

Water is best provided in a gravity bottle—an inverted bottle attached to the side of the enclosure, with a metal "straw" that the animal licks. Change the water every three or four days. The gravity-bottle system is superior to a water bowl that soon becomes filled with litter.

Food should be provided in shallow containers—the metal lid to peanut-butter jar is perfect. Hamsters and gerbils need be fed only once a day, preferably in the early evening. Approximately two tablespoons of regular pelletized chow should suffice. This may be supplemented with fresh salad greens, a little fruit and vegetables, nuts, seeds, cereal grains, raisins, and table scraps—a little egg, cheese, or even meat. Hamsters also enjoy an occasional meal worm or earthworm. Do remember that these are small rodents, and bulky, starchy foods should be avoided. They mostly require high-protein, low-bulk foods, especially the occasional supplements of fresh fruit, salad greens, or raw vegetables.

Handling

To pick up a hamster or gerbil, lay your hand flat in the cage. As it climbs up, or as you slip your hand under it, make the one hand into a cup, and with your other hand form a safe "lid" over the animal. With experience you can learn to pick up a hamster by the scruff of its neck, keeping one hand underneath the animal to prevent its falling. A gerbil should be held instead at the base of its tail—its scruff isn't as loose as a hamster's and you could hurt the neck itself. When suddenly excited, or while being handled, some gerbils tip onto one side and have a mild seizure. This should be no cause for alarm: it is an inherited abnormality. Animals known to be susceptible should be kept quiet and handled very gently.

General Care

Both hamsters and gerbils are rodents: their front, or incisor, teeth grow constantly. The teeth may need trimming with nail clippers or small wire cutters if they get too long and interfere with eating. Check their growth regularly. A piece of hard wood to chew on in the cage helps keep the teeth trimmed naturally. Hamsters and gerbils don't need to be bathed or brushed. They groom themselves and keep their coats smooth and glossy. A poor coat—matted, or shedding—could mean that the pet is sick. With a humidity of fifty percent or more, a gerbil's coat will stand out and look matted. This is no cause for alarm; but ideally they should be kept in as dry an environment as possible.

There are a number of diseases to which hamsters and gerbils are prone. Once you recognize that your pet is sick, waste no time in taking it to your vet. Signs of ill health include lethargy, inactivity, refusal to eat, lack of coordination, discharge from the eyes or nose, or loose stools— "wet tail." Loss of fur may be caused by skin infection or parasites. Wounds caused by scratching or biting may be self-inflicted as the arrival seeks to relieve underlying skin irritation; but if another hamster or gerbil is housed in the same cage, don't overlook the possibility of fighting.

Bite wounds and scabs, especially located around the rump, are a good indicator of pair conflict. The combatants should be placed in separate cages. A hamster that defeats another often marks the loser with its own urine. The latter will flee when it smells the scent marks of the winner (even if the winner is not present).

I recall one winter day going to the garden shed to attend to my hamster colony. I discovered that the heater had broken down. Suzie, my oldest hamster, didn't come out of her nest when I called her. She lay in a tight ball, cold as ice. Dead, I thought: Suzie, my first and oldest hamster, one of Mr. Hobson's show winners, who had produced so many babies. Sadly, I took her indoors.

Then I remembered that hamsters in the wild hibernate when it gets cold. Slowly we brought her around. It was the last time she would hibernate. The heater was fixed at once. I didn't want all my hamsters to go to sleep on me for the winter!

Illnesses and Other Problems

Wet-tail disease is a serious problem in hamsters; the loose stools are indicative of an enteric infection. Veterinary treatment should be sought at once. Like guinea pigs, hamsters are highly sensitive to penicillin; it should never be given. Penicillin destroys gram positive bacteria in the intestines and if used will rapidly lead to a gram negative bacterial enterotoxemia, an often fatal disease.

After a heat period, a female hamster has a creamy vaginal discharge. This is quite normal and no cause for alarm.

All rodents tend to have rather concentrated urine. In rabbits and hamsters it sometimes appears cloudy or turbid. This is due to the formation of crystals in the urine, and is quite normal.

Another occasional cause of alarm is a bloody-looking crust that may develop around the eyes of gerbils. This is a natural secretion (iron porphyrin) from the Harderian gland of the eye.

Breeding

Hamsters can breed as early as four to six weeks of age.

But it is best to allow them to mature and attain at least ten weeks before they are bred.

Because the female is more aggressive than the male, she should be placed in his cage; the entire process should be carefully supervised to prevent injury to the male. Early evening is an ideal time to try this.

The female has a heat cycle every fourth or fifth day; her readiness to breed may be manifested by a raised tail or hind end, especially following a touch or stroke on the rump. This is called the lordosis response. The male hamster sometimes seizes the female's neck scruff in his teeth prior to mating. Remove the female as soon as she has been bred. If breeding hasn't occurred and she is friendly toward the male, some people leave them together a night or two.

It is easy to tell if a female is going to have babies. Her abdomen will swell and her teats will become enlarged. Gestation lasts sixteen days. Near the expected date of delivery, and for at least a week afterward, the mother should not be handled or disturbed. A frightened mother may kill its babies. The young caretaker must be satisfied to hear the mews and peeps of the babies from deep within the nest. Both hamster and gerbil mothers eat the afterbirth, the placental birth tissues of the offspring. The litter will usually number six or seven babies, which are born hairless and blind. The cage and contents should be cleaned thoroughly when the offspring are about two weeks old. Weaning takes place at around twenty-four days of age, after which the young can be separated from the mother. They should be sexed at this time, and males and females kept in separate cages from about five weeks of age to prevent early or unwanted matings. Like-sex groups can be kept together as long as no fighting breaks out.

Gerbils

Unlike the hamster, which is solitary when mature, the gerbil is a gregarious rodent. Several will live peaceably

Gentle gerbil—and curious too.

together as a family, provided the cage is not overcrowded. Gerbils are not exclusively nocturnal, but active in the daytime and often at night too.

The above accounts of caging, feeding, and socializing hamsters holds largely true for gerbils as well. But there are some important differences.

The pet-store gerbil originated in the deserts of Mongolia and is related to the jerboa, or desert rat. Its life expectancy is from two to four years, about a year longer than a hamster. It will not bite unless seriously mishandled, and makes an ideal pet for children. Since the gerbil has been domesticated for some twenty years less than hamsters, varieties in color or coat have not yet been developed (although recently black and spotted mutants have been reported). All gerbils are agouti-colored—brown fur with cream undersides, and long hairy tails ending in a little dark tuft. They have a habit of sitting up on their haunches and looking around like a kangaroo; sometimes they leap quite high. (Some people call them "pocket kangaroos.") A cover is needed, therefore, if they are to be kept in the cage.

Their intense curiosity is a source of constant delight to a young child. Combined with their docile nature, this has made them extremely popular in schools.

Because they are naturally so sociable, they should never be housed alone. It is best to keep two females or a male and female together; avoid pairing males since gerbil males are more aggressive than females (the reverse of the hamster). (Sexing is easy—males have a greater distance between the anus and genital orifice than females.) Ideally a male and female should be paired by eight weeks of age: if left until twelve weeks, they may live together amicably but never breed! To keep a pair from breeding constantly— which they will do after attaining three months of age—a kind way of separating them is to place a half-inch wire screen in the cage as a divider. They still are able to touch, smell, and see each other easily. Females are selective in their choice of a mate, often refusing to breed with a strange male if previously mated with another.

The gestation period is twenty-four days. From four to ten babies are produced in a litter. It is quite safe to leave the father with the mother throughout pregnancy. The family may remain together until the young are twenty-one days old. Young may be weaned then and placed in a separate cage. This is an important step: their mother can produce another litter twenty-four days after the birth of the first!

A female gerbil may go into a pseudo pregnancy; this usually lasts about sixteen days. Delayed implantation—an extraordinary phenomenon—also occurs in these rodents: a fertilized egg may not be implanted into the wall of the uterus for several days, thus increasing the length of time after mating until the offspring will be born. A female, for example, "delays" giving birth for anywhere up to forty-two days if she is mated while nursing a litter!

There is much to learn from these rodents about social behavior, the behavioral development of the young, their body language "displays"—like the foot-drumming and tail vibration threats of the gerbil.

Both have scent-marking glands to mark their territories. Gerbils have a gland on their chests and hamsters have a gland on each flank as well. Some people mistake these for some kind of skin disease!

With hamsters and gerbils readily available and so easy to keep, there's no reason why any child should be deprived of having an animal companion. If not a cat or dog, then why *not* a hamster or gerbil?

17

Rats and Mice

RATS AND MICE make excellent pets. They are usually docile, easy to handle, and do not require any specialized knowledge to keep them healthy. Indeed, one of their few undesirable traits is their reproductive vigor, for a breeding pair of rats or mice will produce a veritable tribe of descendants within a few months.

Mice are generally more popular than rats because they are smaller and cuter-looking. Rats suffer from the bad reputation of their successful wild cousins, but there is no reason to equate the domesticated rat with viciousness, cunning, or the spreading of diseases such as ratbite jaundice and plague. Tame rats are quiet and gentle creatures, often more intelligent and sociable toward their caretakers than mice. Some people don't like their snakelike tails or their quick movements when alarmed, but these are purely subjective reactions. Parents who feel revulsion toward such creatures shouldn't deny their children the opportunity to care for and understand rats and mice. We also owe a great deal to them for some thirty million mice and ten million rats are used each year in laboratories in developing new drugs and in testing substances for consumer safety.

MICE

Pet mice come from the wild housemouse, *Mus musculus*. Mice are good pets not only because they are docile, but because they are economical to keep and very hardy little creatures as well. Male mice produce a strong "mousy" odor, and in order to control this, the young owner should clean out the cages and put in fresh bedding each day. Only too often parents banish mice to an outdoor shed or patio, and the child loses interest in them and does not take adequate care of them. With insufficient bedding, the animals may suffer from exposure, and if not in a safe place, be subjected to the dexterous attempts of a neighborhood cat to break into their cage and eat them. So the first rule is that the mice should be in a safe, warm place, away from drafts. They also should be kept out of direct sunlight.

There are many varieties, or strains, of mice, and countless color variants, from black to Swiss albino, agouti, cinnamon, yellow, piebald, black and white "Dutch," gray, steel-blue, or silver. Most pet mice are of mixed pedigree and don't usually breed true which means that the offspring may have different coat colors.

Mice live an average of one to two years; three years is exceptional. They are, like most rodents, nocturnal, so the best play time is in the evening. One way mouse owners can help reduce the stress of disrupting their sleep patterns is to keep them in a darkened place during the day and give them a light during the night. This way their night will coincide with our day so that the young owner can enjoy them when they are most active. A good plan for a small rodent colony is to set a timer-switch for white light between 7:00 p.m. and 7:00 a.m., then for the day, switching to a red light (which they can't see) so they can be observed during their simulated night time.

Cages

Caging must above all be secure, for mice will chew their way out of a poorly constructed cage and soon colonize the house. An aquarium or shoebox-shaped rodent cage of plastic or metal, with a wire mesh lid, is ideal. Bedding should be provided in the form of sawdust, wood shavings, or ground corncobs. Nesting material such as hay, paper towels, or shredded newspaper is necessary for breeding pairs. The litter and uneaten food should be cleaned out every day and fresh material put down. Cage and fixtures should be scoured and scrubbed clean every three or four weeks. There should be sufficient cage space to allow for a running wheel, which mice enjoy and which most pet stores carry.

Mice also like ramp-ladders and elevated runways or platforms and especially like having a nest box above the ground. If you are good at carpentry, such additions in the mouse cage would make their world more fun for them and more enjoyable for you as you observe them going about their business.

Food and Water

Water should be dispensed via an inverted gravity water bottle attached to one inside edge of the cage or tank. The nipple should be low enough for the mice to be able to lick. This is better than having a water dish in the cage. Fresh water should be given every day. Food can be given either via a wire food-hopper for dry mouse-chow or in a shallow container on the floor of the cage. Mice enjoy a variety of foods, including raw vegetables and fruit (not too much or their stools may become runny), cereals such as granola or rolled oats, natural breakfast cereals, cat or puppy chow, whole wheat bread or toast, boiled egg, cheese, and nuts. They do not need vitamin supplements, and fruit and vegetables are nonessential treats.

Breeding

Mice are ready to breed as early as six weeks of age, and have a natural heat cycle every four to five days. Nineteen to twenty-one days after mating, the female gives birth to as many as ten or more blind and hairless babies. It is a good idea to leave mother and offspring as undisturbed as possible during the first week, although, unlike hamsters, mice will rarely cannibalize their babies. Offspring can be weaned at twenty-one days. The male can be left safely with his family, as can other mice—even another mother who is nursing her own litter. But while females usually live peaceably together, having more than one male in the cage could lead to fighting. Bite wounds, especially at the base of the tail, are a tell-tale sign.

Pregnancies can be "timed" in mice. Females housed together tend to go out of heat and do not cycle, but as soon as a male is put with them, up to fifty percent will be in heat within three days. Another interesting phenomenon is called the Bruce effect. If a pregnant female is exposed to a strange male any time during the first four days after mating, the original pregnancy may be blocked and she will have no offspring. Also intriguing is the fact that a mouse will have a heat period just after she has delivered a litter. If she is bred then, she will give birth to another litter twenty-five to thirty days later. Instead of the usual gestation of from nineteen to twenty-one days, the "incubation" period is extended, probably so she can finish nursing her first litter before the next one arrives. This is called delayed implantation.

Mice have other fascinating qualities. Their rapid and fastidious grooming is a delight to observe. They also enjoy grooming one another. Mothers will retrieve their young when danger threatens, just like a mother cat. Mice have a threat display in which they rear up on their hind legs and rattle, or vibrate their tails. They are adept climbers and explorers, and all kinds of mazes, tunnels, and the like can be set up to test their learning abilities. Mice make few audible sounds; one is a squeak of alarm. "Pups," as the infants are called, emit ultrasonic calls inaudible to the human ear but which will make the mother tend them or find and retrieve one that has crawled out of the nest.

Illnesses

Mice have few diseases, and sickness is rare if they are adequately cared for. Mites may cause some skin problems, but adding twenty percent in cedar chips to the bedding is said to help reduce the problem. Putting a Vapona strip over the cage for twenty-four hours will also help. Ectromelia (mouse pox) and Tyzzer's disease are rare but lethal mouse-specific diseases. Diarrhea and pneumonia may be caused by a variety of infections. Generally, adding a little Terramycin or Chloromycetin to the drinking water will remedy such problems. Salmonellosis is one disease in mice that may be transmitted to man, but fortunately it is rare today.

Handling

The most common problem for humans is the danger of being bitten. Rabies shots are not needed, but bites should be washed and disinfected. For deeper bites (and especially from pet rats) an anti-tetanus shot may be indicated. By handling the mice regularly and gently and not disturbing them prior to picking them up, you can best assure that you will not be bitten. Most mice are so docile that biting is rare, but a scared mouse, or one that smells food on your hand, may nip. Mice only bite when they are afraid, and that is usually because the handler has been too quick, rough, or nervous in scooping up and holding the creature. With a mouse that is difficult to catch, seize it by the *base* of the tail between fingers and thumb and scoop the other hand under it so it will be secure. Then you may release the tail and hold it in the cup of your two hands. Never attempt to seize the mouse by the end of its tail—in some mice the skin of the tail comes off when grasped. This is possibly a protective alarm reaction, much like that of some lizards whose tails may break off to allow the animal to escape the grip of a predator.

RATS

Close cousins of mice, rats also make interesting and entertaining pets. Like mice, they are nocturnal. All pet rats are derived from the Norwegian rat, *Rattus norwegicus*. Their longevity is greater than that of mice—up to three or four years. There are fewer color variations. The common varieties are the Sprague-Dawley, the Wistar White, and the Long-Evans brown—black-and-white "hooded" rat. The Sprague-Dawley and the Wistar are easier to handle. Generally, rats are much more docile and sociable toward their caretakers than mice. Tests have shown that rats can recognize familiar handlers, and they will engage in various forms of play such as exploring novel things and even collecting or retrieving transportable materials, like string.

Cages

The jaws of rats are more powerful than those of mice, and rats can quickly gnaw their way out of a wooden box cage. Metal or smooth plastic is better; a large glass aquarium is a good choice. The top should be secured down so the animals cannot push their way out, and should be of perforated metal or wire mesh for ventilation. Perhaps the most characteristic trait of rats is their curiosity—they love to explore and manipulate—and so their cages should be as large as possible, say one foot by two or three feet. It should contain runways, tunnels, and ramps for climbing up and over; in and out. Rats do not, however, enjoy the activity wheel as much as mice do. The basic care, handling, feeding, and watering of mice also holds true for rats. Because front incisor teeth of rats grow constantly, it is a good idea to give them some wood in the cage to gnaw on, otherwise their teeth will have to be trimmed as they overgrow and get out of line.

Domestication has reduced much of the ancestral wildness and aggressiveness of rats so that several members of the same sex can be housed together. In the wild, rats live in "clans," and are extremely territorial and aggressive toward strange intruding rats.

Handling

The more often a pet rat is handled, the more tractable it will become. Some will respond when called, especially if they are rewarded with a favorite tidbit. A rat should be picked up by slowly scooping with both hands, and can be held securely around the chest, with the thumb under its chin to prevent twisting. As with mice, a rat will slip the skin off its tail if picked up in that way.

Breeding

Rats can breed as early as age forty days, but it is advisable to allow the female to mature up to three months of age before breeding her. Most mothers will build elaborate nests before they deliver, and ample nesting material should be provided, as well as a small nest box. Gestation lasts some twenty-one days, and the offspring can be weaned at three weeks. They should be separated into groups of the same sex after weaning in order to avoid early breeding. As with mice, the female rat has a heat just after she gives birth, and also has a delayed implantation mechanism. It is not advisable to keep another female in a nursing mother's cage, but the male may be left in (if you don't mind having more babies), and he will take an active role in looking after the babies. Unlike mice, rats continue to grow when they reach adulthood, which accounts for the great size that old ones attain.

Rats have a rich and easy-to-read repertoire of body language "displays," ranging from submissive crouching for grooming to a vertical, tooth-chattering threat posture. They have a friendly, "crawling-under-a-companion" behavior, engage in mutual grooming, playful wrestling, and hoarding of food and "toys." Females sometimes show an elaborate courtship dance, and males have a postcourtship song at ultrasonic frequency. Rats in groups will sometimes develop a dominance hierarchy or "pecking order," with a leader, or alpha rat (who is often the largest), and a bottom-of-the-rung omega.

Don't be alarmed or revolted if you see your rat sitting up like a squirrel and eating one of its stools. Mice and other rodents do this, and it is perfectly natural. This is called refection or coprophagia, which the animal does in order to obtain essential nutrients from the action of bacteria in its droppings.

Illnesses

Healthy and well-cared-for rats rarely develop any serious illnesses. Chronic respiratory diseases—sniffles and inflamed eyes—require antibiotic medication of the drinking water. Sometimes an upper respiratory infection may involve the ear labyrinth or balancing organ, and the rat will have a twisted head and tend to walk in circles. Rats will occasionally develop a viral eye infection which causes the eyeball and cheek to puff out. There is no specific treatment, but it is a good idea to protect the eye with ophthalmic ointment. Most rats recover from this problem within a couple of weeks. Older rats may tear a brown-red secretion from each eye, giving the appearance of having red tears. This is a natural secretion and is no cause for alarm. The rat may, in the course of grooming itself, coincidentally spread this secretion over its neck and shoulders, giving its coat a reddish-brown tint.

Rats and mice are fascinating creatures and easy to care for, and any child who is interested in keeping and raising animals should begin with them. Rats and/or mice can also be a focal point for catalyzing classroom activities and discussions around the school menagerie. The dramatic reproductive capacity of mice, for example, can give the children an immediate grasp of what reproduction and overpopulation mean. Exposure to such innocuous and intelligent creatures early in life can do much to allay the irrational prejudice and squeamishness toward rats and mice that so many acquire. To have kept and studied them is to establish a bridge of understanding and appreciation which can only help our regard for and relationships with other animals later in life.

18

Rabbits and Guinea Pigs

OTHER THAN KEEPING the occasional spider, pollywog, lizard, or caterpillar (which either escaped or expired mysteriously), I was about four years old before I had a "real animal of my own." Four or so may be the ideal age for starting a young child off with a first animal companion. When I was a child, though, kindergartens and grade schools had no animal menageries the likes of which are seen in many today. Come spring back then pussywillow catkins, sprouting cress and beans, and jam jars of frog spawn and pollywogs adorned school windowsills. And it was springtime when two Easter bunnies visited me—and one came to stay.

We housed him in a hutch my father built in a sheltered place in our back garden. That rabbit was my first "animal teacher," opening up for me a fascination and continuing interest and concern for our animal kin. Ironically, my friend Albert's parents next door raised many rabbits for their meat. I won't forget the day his older sister came over wearing Angora rabbit fur mittens from one of their rabbits! To each his own, but I knew even then that I could never eat or wear my rabbit friend. When he did finally die, he had a fitting funeral and was buried under the rhododendron bushes at the end of the garden.

Rabbits have been domesticated since about 1000 B.C. There are now many varieties: the large New Zealand white and Flemish giant can weigh fifteen pounds, the Polish weigh only about three. The Dutch rabbit has a distinctive white belt around its chest and neck, while its head and posterior may be black, blue, brown, red, or gray. The Himalayan and Californian rabbits are, respectively, white with smudges of black on the nose and feet, and white with dark brown ears and paws (like a Siamese cat). A long-haired variety, the Angora, needs daily grooming; it was once raised extensively for its fur, which was used widely in the felt-hat industry. There are also English, Havana, long blue-haired chinchilla, short velvety Rex, and pendulous-eared lop rabbit varieties. And rabbit fanciers have developed—and are still creating—new varieties. The life expectancy of a rabbit ranges from five to ten years.

The size of a rabbit's cage should vary according to the kind of rabbit you have. Ideally the cage or hutch should be three to five feet long and one-and-one-half to two feet wide and high; it must be larger if you want to breed a doe (female). There should be two compartments: one with plenty of hay and room for a nesting space; it should be covered and have ventilation holes only, so that it is dark and quiet. The adjacent compartment can be open and provided with a wire mesh door.Many people prefer rabbit cages with a wire mesh floor so that the urine and droppings fall through and are collected in a pan beneath the hutch. There are two reasons not to use such a cage. Rabbits eat their own droppings, taking them in as part of their normal digestive process in order to obtain B vitamins created by the action of intestinal bacteria in the droppings the first time around. This behavior—common in many rodents—is quite normal, and is termed pseudo-rumination or *refection*. The second reason is that a rough wire surface may cause some rabbits to develop sore hocks, a painful chronic infection of the long soles on their hind feet. If the wire mesh is smooth and the grid not too small, or if a slatted wooden floor is used instead, these two problems may be avoided. However, many rabbit owners go in for a solid floor and a litter tray filled with sawdust, since rabbits designate one area of the outer compartment of their hutch as their toilet.

The enclosure can be kept in a garage, or outdoors in a shaded, draught-free place. Cover the front of the cage with a board on cold nights and provide extra nest hay in the winter. A waterproof roof of tarpaper, or other suitable material, is essential. The hutch should be built on legs, raised about three feet above the ground. This should help keep marauding animals (especially cats) at a distance. A frightened doe will kill her infants. Guinea pigs, too, panic if a strange animal is near.

Because rabbits naturally use a specific area for their toilet, they can be housebroken. (In the wild, each rabbit burrow has its own communal latrine.) A litter tray could be located in a convenient out-of-the-way spot—similar to that for a cat—and a nest box constructed for the rabbit to sleep in.

Does pull out fur to line their nests when the time approaches to give birth. Not many mammals will provide such a comfortable nest. Such fur, naturally, should not be cleaned out.

Food and Water

Some people claim that rabbits need no water. Indeed they do! The tidiest way is to use the gravity water bottle. Drops of water come forth only when the rabbit licks the metal tube, as it soon learns to do. (The same method is ideal for guinea pigs. Guinea pigs, however, have a habit of blowing air back up the sipper tube. This is why the water becomes quickly discolored and needs replenishing quite often.) If the rabbit is kept in the house, a heavy, nontipping bowl of water will do. Food should be provided in a similar heavy, steady dish to prevent spillage and waste.

The diets for rabbits and guinea pigs are virtually identical. Rabbit pellets, consisting mainly of dried alfalfa, form an excellent and complete balanced diet; hay, freshly cut grass trimmings (upon which there is no weed killer!) and cut-up pieces of any root vegetable add variety. Occasional apple slices, salad greens, and wild plants—dock and dandelion—are excellent treats, and good for the pet, too.

Never feed your guinea pig rabbit pellets, vegetables, or other food without also providing plenty of hay or dried grass. (Store some good quality grass trimmings for the winter.) The little animals need the roughage; and some unknown factor in hay is said to be an essential component of their diet. Hay to nibble on and play with may also help reduce the problem of "barbering"—in other words, it will stop them from pulling fur, their own and other animals'.

Guinea pigs, like monkeys and people, are unable to synthesize Vitamin C themselves. They are dependent upon an external source. A half-gram tablet of Vitamin C in a litre of water will suffice if their feed is not fortified with Vitamin C; replenish this fresh each day.

Handling

Never pick a rabbit up by the ears, like the magician producing one from his top hat. The ears may be damaged if you try—and the rabbit may well kick or bite to show its displeasure and pain. The ears may be held to secure the rabbit in place while you reach the other hand under its belly. The best way is to hold its strong hind feet with one hand; then pass the fingers of the other hand around and over its shoulders.

Socialized rabbits enjoy being petted and will respond when called. But, as with other animals, rabbits are sociable and highly responsive only if subject to frequent human contact early in life.

A poorly socialized rabbit is more likely to bite the hand that feeds it than a well-socialized one. And beware a doe tending her young— as you would expect (but might forget upon seeing her bunnies), does are more defensive at such times.

Rabbits have a clear and varied repertoire of signals that the owner should learn to recognize. A sudden jump to face you, sometimes accompanied by a sharp expiratory grunt and thumping a hind foot on the ground, is a threat. Lying low, ears back and eyes half closed, is a submissive, friendly signal. Young rabbits enjoy chase and tag games: this is something to try with a young, well-socialized rabbit that won't mistake your intentions and be frightened instead. Some rabbits even like to play ball, and hide and seek!

Breeding

Think twice. If you produce more rabbits, can you find homes for them? Are you going to eat them instead? There's no trick to breeding rabbits, but follow two important rules. First, place the doe in the buck's hutch, *never* the other way around. The pair may be left together for six to eight days. After that, the doe becomes increasingly intolerant of the buck. Hence rule two! He should then be removed. He should not be left with the family.

During the spring and summer a mature doe comes into heat every three weeks, and is sexually receptive for three to four days. At such times she will be restless, sometimes rolling onto her back and exhibiting swollen and discolored hindquarters. The doe is a reflex ovulator: when she is in heat and is mated, the stimulation by the male triggers the ovaries to shed their eggs, insuring a fertile mating.

The courtship behavior is fascinating to observe. Courtship chasing often occurs, during which the male "display" with a stiff-legged gait, hindquarters raised, and with the tail raised up and forward—tail flagging. He may spray the female with his urine; this is called *epuresis* and occurs sometimes during fights between rival rabbits. He may also rub his chin gland on the female's back to mark her with his scent. Sometimes the male seizes the female's back to mark her with his scent. Sometimes the male seizes the female's shoulder fur in his teeth. A receptive female will eventually "stand" for the male and raise her hindquarters—this is called *lordosis*. As in most rodents, following mating a plug of dried semen remains in the vagina (the so-called vaginal plug).

The female begins to make a nest about two weeks after a successsful mating. The first stage of the nest is made of straw or hay. Near the time of delivery, when her belly fur loosens, she will line it with fur.

The gestation period is twenty-eight to thirty-two days. The babies are born blind, deaf, and hairless. An unusual aspect of rabbit mothering is the fact that the doe nurses her offspring for only about five minutes once every twenty-four hours. So don't worry if she doesn't seem to spend very much time in the nest with her babies!

Unlike most rodents, rabbits do not retrieve babies that stray from the nest; probably because deep in the burrow, the babies would be unable to stray very far. Never interfere with the nest: listen but don't look or touch, as the doe may kill the babies if she is disturbed. Wait to look at them until they emerge from the nest themselves; they will then be two to three weeks old. Then give them plenty of gentle handling to get them used to people. They may be weaned after six weeks of age and then separated from the mother and put into a "playpen" or large hutch. Sexes should be segregated at three months of age to prevent unwanted breeding. Females should not be bred until they are fully mature—from six to nine months, depending on the breed. While the doe is lactating, she will be receptive to a buck, and if she has a small litter, she may well conceive another; keep males away while she is nursing if no more offspring are desired.

In the wild, rabbits live in "warrens"—groups of three to six amicable females and two or three males inhabiting a complex series of burrows. The males are more aggressive than the females and have a well-defined "pecking order" or hierarchy; as adults, they are best not housed together, because they somehow injure each other in rivalry fights, and may even castrate each other. Interestingly, female rabbits housed together tend to go into a state of false preg-

handsome, trainable
bit. Notice the im-
ssive dewlap.

A lop-eared rabbit—one
of many varieties.

nancy: to breed one, she should be isolated from the others for three weeks so that she will come into heat and be receptive.

Illnesses

Rabbits are very susceptible to respiratory infections: at the first sign of sniffles or swollen eyes a rabbit should be taken for veterinary treatment. They are also prone to getting ear mites, sore hocks (described earlier), and various dysenteric forms of diarrhea or "wet tail" (especially coccidiosis), any of which should receive the prompt attention of a veterinarian. Home doctoring should be avoided. Rabbit "snuffles," as the name implies, is an upper respiratory infection often caused by pasteurella; early veterinary treatment will prevent further complications. Rabbits, in addition, are particularly susceptible to heat stroke—they should be provided with shelter that is cool, and shaded in the summer.

GUINEA PIGS

Housing

Also called cavies, guinea pigs originated in South America and were taken by the Spaniards from Peru to Guinea. Natives there raised them for food. (Although they were known as "little pigs," they are not related to the pig, of course!)

They come with many different coat colors and types—from smooth white, black, piebald, and tricolored to the rosetted whorled coat of the "Abyssinian" cavy, and the long-haired Peruvian. They enjoy a relatively long life expectancy from six to eight years.

A hutch similar to that described for a rabbit is ideal. Several adult guinea pigs can be housed together with less trouble than with rabbits. They are very sociable, gregarious rodents. Some people even build them a walk-in A-frame shed; like the hutch, this has an outer wire-walled run and an inner, solid-walled nesting area. Always provide a solid floor—not a wire mesh floor, on which they may easily break a leg.

The "harem" situation is a good social unit: a boar (the male) may be housed with three or four sows. Males tend to be aggressive among each other, so it is unwise to house two adult boars together with females. Provide them with cardboard boxes or drain-pipe segments to play in—but *not* ramps or ledges such as you might arrange for mice or gerbils. Cavies, having such heavy bodies and delicate legs, can injure themselves easily in a fall.

Provide them with plenty of sawdust litter or newspaper. The cage should be cleaned out daily. Unlike the rabbit, a guinea pig makes its toilet wherever he happens to be! If you like, you can arrange to have a portable hutch, placing the floor of the outer compartment on your lawn in the summer. The animals enjoy being on the grass and will keep that spot on your lawn trimmed and fertilized. But avoid hot places in direct sunlight.

Handling

The same rules for handling a rabbit hold for guinea pigs. Since they don't have long ears, seize them around the shoulders with one hand; as you lift the animal up, cup your other hand under its hind legs to support the body weight. As is the case with other animals, the earlier in life they are first handled, the better socialized they will be. They are, naturally, very docile animals and very rarely attempt to bite. Like rabbits, they enjoy being petted and groomed with a brush (essential if you have a long-haired animal).

Breeding

Fathers and mothers can be kept together all the time.

In the wild, many guinea pigs share the same home range. Both males and females have a strict rank or pecking order, which is especially evident while feeding; the highest-ranking males have more or less exclusive breeding rights. There is no need to separate them to stop their breeding; unless, of course, too many babies are being produced. The sow has a ten-hour heat period every thirteen to eighteen days. The boar sometimes seizes the female's neck scruff in his teeth prior to mating. If frustrated, he may also spray her with his urine.

The gestation period is very long—seventy days. Because of this, guinea pigs have small litters—usually one or two offspring—which are highly developed at birth. Because the infants are so nearly mature, the mother need not build a nest. Within a few hours the infants will be nibbling solid food, although the mother continues to nurse them until they are three to four weeks of age. They can be weaned any time after this. Both rabbit and guinea-pig mothers eat the placental afterbirth tissues of the offspring. In addition, the mother guinea pig eats up the excrement of her offspring for four or five days (as do cats and dogs). Infant guinea pigs, like the young of other rodents, often eat the droppings from their mother and from other adults. This seems to be a natural way of inoculating their digestive system with certain bacteria that aid them in assimilating food.

Several sows and their infants can be housed together peaceably. The mother becomes imprinted to the smell and distinctive call of her offspring (and they to her). Because the female can be bred as soon as she has given birth, it is a very good idea to remove the boar for a few days; otherwise he may worry and trample mother and infant in his courtship order. Seventy-five percent of all sows conceive on the first day after giving birth!

The young can be kept together until about six weeks, then they should be segregated if you don't wish them to breed. Sexing them is easy: at the posterior end, the female has a Y-shaped fold; the males have a slit-shaped fold in the

A fluffy guinea pig—which end is which?

center of the scrotum. Females also have a vaginal membrane which remains closed except when they are in heat.

Boars socialized from early life with each other remain sociable. But they will be aggressive toward strange males, or one that has been separated for some time and then is reintroduced.

Illnesses

All vegetables and salads should be thoroughly washed to reduce the possibility of introducing a parasitic or bacterial disease. Moldy foods should never be given. Sudden changes in diet, litter, or bedding should be avoided. Such precautions are especially important with guinea pigs since they are very susceptible to pseudotuberculosis and salmonellosis, infections frequently transmitted by wild birds and rodents and which may contaminate some green foods. It is important to remember that both these are *zoonoses*— they may be transmitted to man. Guinea pigs are very susceptible to stress—when veterinary treatment is needed they should be handled and transported with great care. They should *never* be given penicillin: it is poisonous to this species.

Piggie-whistle and Other Intriguing Traits

The most characteristic behavior of the guinea pig is its whistle call. Try mimicking it and the animal will often respond. It is a social signal and frequently emitted when they are petted and at feeding time.

Wild (and some domesticated) rabbits, primarily bucks, rub their chins against objects; this is a special marking of their territories with a scent gland located under the chin. It has been said that the buck also uses pellets to mark his territory; and he may spray his mates and offspring with his own urine—giving all a social bond of live-together-smell-alike. It has been discovered that a buck subordinate to another male becomes dominant if the two are placed in an enclosure containing the droppings of the subordinate.

The body language of guinea pigs is fascinating to observe. Two males, "facing up" aggressively, chatter their teeth and stamp their hind feet threateningly. The hair along their backs may be erected; with back arched, they may scent-mark the ground by dragging their posteriors—anal glands are located under the tail near the rectum. Males also mark their territories with this *supracaudal*, or tail, gland. In aggressive encounters, males may twist around and extrude their testicles: a flash of dominance, enhanced by a brightly colored scrotum!

The courtship behavior of the male is a delightful sequence of actions. The boar purrs to the female and walks in a waddling-rolling fashion as he follows attentively behind her.

If you are susceptible to allergies, be careful of guinea pigs: they are the worst animals for causing allergies in people. If you get a guinea pig and then get an allergy, you will know why. Asthmatic children should usually avoid contact with and exposure to guinea pigs.

Guinea pigs and rabbits are indeed interesting animals in their own right. Being so easy to keep, they make good companion animals for children. One should never underestimate the benefits to a child of having an animal to care for, to play with, and to understand. A living "presence" in the form of a guinea pig or rabbit will greatly enrich the childhood years.

19

Raising Animals Together

CAN A KITTEN find true happiness with a dog, hamsters, and a parakeet? Is canine fulfillment possible in a home containing gerbils, goldfish, kittens, turtles, and three white mice? And can the multipet owner survive?

Yes, sometimes a variety of pets—and their owners—*can* live together in comparative peace. But problems do arise in such mixed-pet families—not only among the animals themselves, but in the complex interplay of relationships between the owners and the various species of pets.

Don't let that stop you if your family has a yen for a variety of pets or the natural opportunity to raise them in the suburbs or country. If you keep an eye out for certain problems and follow certain guidelines, you can keep harmony in your home menagerie. And it's worth the effort. Life in a multipet family can be a highly rewarding experience.

A Need for Privacy

In nature, multispecies relationships are more the rule than the exception, and animals are quite often dependent upon each other in a given habitat. Deer and chipmunks both will run for cover when they hear the alarm call of a blackbird or squirrel. Different species of bird will club together and mob a predator such as a fox—or your cat. Badgers and coyotes will form hunting partnerships, and although it's hard to imagine such unlikely playmates as a baboon and a gazelle, they have been known to frolic together.

But, although various species of wild animal do exist with a certain degree of harmony, if things get tough, they have plenty of space in which to escape or hide. This is the first element to consider in your own home.

Most animals have a sense of "their own place" and a need for privacy and security. One should therefore provide a safe refuge to which each animal can withdraw. It must be free to get away from the other animals, from family members, and especially from children. This need should be respected at all times, particularly when the pet is vulnerable because of its size or age.

Growing Up Together

Another key to a peaceful mixed-pet family is to raise the different species together. For one thing, young pets are physically incapable of inflicting serious injury on each other. And secondly, being young, they need companionship and play. A puppy and kitten raised together will probably still be friends when both mature. (Animals that play together stay together!)

It is important, however, to supervise the young pets' play—in case it gets too rough—and to discipline a budding bully. This rule holds just as true for dogs of different size and physical strength as it does for a puppy and a kitten, or a kitten paired with a squirrel or chipmunk.

Generally, mammals (animals with fur) will get along very well with each other when raised together. And placing an infant animal in the presence of an older one of a different species will often work out surprisingly well. The in-

Raising animals together can be tricky—especially when they are jealous of each other and want your undivided attention!

(Kathy Garvey, HSUS)

fantile behavior usually inhibits aggressive or predatorial responses from the older animal. Indeed, some dogs will behave maternally toward kittens, young rabbits, opposums, skunks, raccoons, and others.

Not all animals develop at the same rate, however. Chickens, ducklings, horses, guinea pigs, and sheep, for instance, are extremely mature at birth and will develop social attachments during the first day or so. Others, such as puppies, kittens, raccoons, pigeons, and rabbits, may take several weeks before they can socialize. If, for example, you want to raise a dog and a duckling together, the duckling should not be more than two days old or it will be too old to develop an attachment to the dog, whereas the puppy should be four to five weeks old.

The Animal Instinct

There are times when instinct takes over, and even those species that have been closely raised may suddenly become enemies. The prime instinct to watch out for is the prey-chasing, catching, and killing response. The quick movement of a hamster, for instance, may at first elicit a normal play reaction in a cat, but if the rodent is frightened and running away to hide, its behavior may suddenly unleash a predatorial response. Then the play may get rough, and may even be disrupted for good.

These predatorial reactions don't begin to develop until six to eight weeks of age, so if you wish to raise a carnivore, such as a puppy or kitten, with a potential "prey species," such as a squirrel, rabbit, or rodent (gerbil, hamster, guinea pig), you should try introducing them before this age. One easy way to do it is through "cross-fostering," where you place an alien species right in the litter with the mother. It is true that a mother dog or cat may simply not accept a young rabbit or hamster, but it's also possible that you'll witness the remarkable sight of maternal instinct overriding the natural prey-killing instinct! It's risky, of course, but it's one way to keep alive a delicate animal that you might have difficulty raising by yourself.

You must also be alert to the natural signals your animals use when trying to ward off attack, for they may be misread by the other animals. For example, the natural submission gesture of a dog is to roll over onto one side and whine. A rabbit, however, may simply freeze on all fours. Not responding to this as a submissive signal, the dog may continue to be the aggressor, and a quick escape movement by the rabbit may automatically release the dog's prey-killing bite.

A note of caution: If you step into a conflict between your pets, any sudden movement on your part may be interpreted by the animals as a sign that you are joining the attack. This could mean serious injury to you or the other animal. If, for example, your hound is playing too aggressively with the rabbit or pawing the turtle too roughly, say "no" gently but firmly to the dog, placing your hand in its mouth so that it feels your hand and not the rabbit's fur or the turtle's shell. This should make it understand your concern and disapproval.

Love and Sex

A very common consequence of raising different pets together is confusion over sexual imprinting. I have a friend with a rooster that sometimes attempts to mount his cat! Occasionally, a cat may become enamored of a large bird. Even more common is the cat that solicits its dog companion or a small dog that becomes enormously aroused and attached to a companion rabbit or cat. These "attractions" are difficult to avoid, but they should not really worry anyone. If neither animal seems unduly disturbed by the overtures of the other. I would curb my own distaste and let things be. No offspring can result, since such species are generally incompatible. But these unconsummated sexual relationships do show how profoundly early attachments influence later sexual preferences.

Jealousy can also be a problem in a mixed-pet family. Just as a dog will become jealous if a canine companion is getting a lot of attention, so it may sulk when a kitten, bunny, skunk or raccoon is getting more than its share. Once an animal has grown up with an alien species, it will relate to it in much the same way as it would to a member of its own species. Jealousy, sibling rivalry, and possessiveness over food, play objects, or a favorite sofa or corner must be carefully supervised, because it is then that the natural inhibitions resulting from early socialization can break down. A rabbit would obviously have very little defense against the teeth of a dog. You should be very much on guard when showing excessive affection to one animal while ignoring the other. In the mixed-pet home, as in the home with more than one child, affection must be spread out equally.

Loners and Groupies

The need for continuing companionship does vary among different species. A "groupie" such as a dog, a herd animal such as a goat, or a clan species such as a rabbit tends to sustain close bonds of kinship throughout life. But some species become more solitary as they reach maturity. The domestic cat is one of these; and the raccoon, the fox, and the skunk also feel an increasing need for personal freedom as they grow older. This difference can cause conflict in a mixed-pet home, unless space to retreat to is provided for the more solitary animal.

I know a family who have a beautiful gray fox that only comes out to socialize in the evening, spending the day alone in the quiet basement. When younger, the fox would stay in the kitchen with the household cats and dogs; its detachment from them grew with age. One should respect these differences and not force the less gregarious animals to be social; otherwise their frustration may provoke aggressive reactions.

Food Conflicts

One psychologist who experimented with raising different species together found that conflicts occurred over food. By carefully supervising his animals at feeding time, when the animals were still young, he was able to condition the animals to eat together peacefully.

For the average pet owner, it's enough to be aware that trouble can erupt at mealtime and keep a sharp watch. Remember, however, this friction is just as likely between two cats or two dogs as between a cat and a pet raccoon. It's clearly advisable to feed all animals at the same time—but in different places. One possibility is to restrict access of one pet to the food of the other, such as feeding your cat or raccoon on a high counter away from the dog's reach.

Ranking Order

In families with gregarious pets, you can see the development of a very clear social hierarchy, or rank order. In one family I know, the rooster, a very fine fellow indeed, rules over a group of five cats and three dogs (each with its own very clear rank) and, occasionally, even the master and mistress. You may wonder why a very large dog or a powerful cat would bow in submission or respectfully get off a sofa when an apparently weaker species like the rooster decides to move in. But physical power alone is not always the deciding factor. Are we perhaps dealing with a greater mental energy? Or with some psychic power that animals are able to detect and respect? For me, such fascinating possibilities open up the entire question of the superiority or inferiority of various species, including man.

20

Wild Animals as Pets

WHEN A CHILD sees something he likes he immediately wants to have it. Grownups, despite their best resolutions and the lessons of experience, often follow their more childish impulses and finish up with a lemon or white elephant of some sort. Worse, they sometimes end up with a wild animal they thought would make a pet.

Movies and TV programs are generally misleading in their portrayal of wild animals—especially those romantic/ tragic Disneyesque fantasies (for such they are) about a boy befriending a cougar, wolf, eagle, whatever, in the wild. From childhood our heads are so crammed with such confusing fact and fiction that it's easy to be taken in by a pet store or wild-animal ranch offering appealing, interesting young wild animals. The list of wild animals for sale reads like an inventory from a latter-day Noah's ark: parrots, falcons, tropical fish, turtles, tarantulas, lizards, lion cubs, and cubs of fox, wolf, bobcat, skunk (de-scented), and types of monkeys ranging from squirrel monkey to capuchin. Each one has its distinctive qualities: rare, exotic, beautiful, dangerous; such a variety that the idiosyncratic tastes of all would-be owners can be satisfied.

Before and since Josephine Baker paraded down the

Champs Elysées leading (or being led by) a brace of cheetahs, people in the entertainment world have enjoyed the
added status and glamour of owning a wild animal, along
with the resultant attention. Others flaunt clothing made of
the valuable fur or skin of such animals. Football teams and
college fraternities have their mascots—goats, bears, lions.
Advertising companies keep trained wild animals available
for product promotions. Add to this exposure the frequent
natural-history TV documentaries exposing us to all manner of wild life, and our national mania for the new and different, and it is little wonder that the ownership of wild
animals is increasing by leaps and bounds—or by snarls and
hisses.

Wild animals *do not* make pets, and having one often
ends in tragedy—the animal is donated to a zoo or, more
usually, is destroyed. Few animals can be released again
into the wild after a life in captivity. Even fewer accept
their own kind or breed after being raised more or less exclusively with man. No zoo wants a full-grown chimpanzee, wolf, or lion that can't be reintegrated with its own
kind—no one wants such an animal.

People have had to give up their wild pets for a variety of
reasons, but basically it is because the animals have not
been domesticated. Wild animals have unreliable temperaments, are fearful of strangers or sudden noises, and unpredictable and often aggressive during the breeding season.

If, like a wolf, an animal has an inborn tendency to respond to a leader (its "master"), it runs with an easy-to-
manage flock or herd, it may easily be controlled and ultimately domesticated by man. Less gregarious species—
especially wild cats and raccoons, which do not form packs
or herds—are less easily domesticated or tamed. The natural mother-infant bond can be replaced if the owner takes
on the parental role when the animal is still very young. If
the wild animal's bond with its parents remains close even
as an adult, then it should remain attached as an adult to its
human foster parent, who becomes "leader" rather than
"parent." Most wild species of reptile, bird, and mammal

A young raccoon, tractable, curious, and playful. It's the ideal pet at this age, but in a few months it will probably be wild and unreliable and will have to be set free, and its chances of survival are slim.

break with parents, often following some conflict and rivalry aggression before they reach maturity; as adults they do not respond to a "leader," because they are so independent; nor will they learn to. Thus, the primary social bond with the human foster parent breaks with maturity (in raccoons, foxes, and most wild cat species) and does not endure in the more gregarious species, such as the wolf or rhesus monkey.

One complication of being a foster parent is that the animal may become sexually attached to you. It may also pose difficulties because of special dietary requirements. But a more common oversight at the outset is the question of what will happen if it gets sick. Less is known about the diseases that wild animals may get and so subject to—and, to begin with, less is known about the health, dietary requirements, and diseases of wild animals than of domesticated animals. I've seen monkeys crippled by inadequate diets. Others contract a disease, like T.B., which can be transmitted and infect the owner—so they are destroyed. Innocent little terrapins were recently outlawed and now can't be sold in pet stores because they can transmit salmonellosis, a severe internal disease, to man. Some wild animals literally go "cage crazy," being unable to adapt to a lifetime of confinement.

A woman in St. Louis kept a mountain lion in her dark basement until the Humane Society came in and had the animal removed to a zoo. A cheetah in New York mutilated a baby's feet—the baby's booties were made of rabbit fur! In Colorado a bitch wolf nearly killed her handler—he didn't know she had just given birth to a litter of cubs and that he was seen as a threat to the infants. A few years ago in Hollywood a film star was mauled by a lion alarmed by some mobile camera equipment. A writer lost half her hand while fondling a "pet" raccoon. Another writer had to destroy her coyote when it went crazy in its cage for "no apparent reason" and would not allow anyone to approach. I could continue for a long time with such stories.

Wild animals possess no artifice—their actions are trying

Fun for a while, but a skunk (even de-scented) is a skunk and never will be a suitable pet. *(Lucinda Dowell, HSUS)*

to tell us something. The problem is simply this: thousands of years of domestication, entailing selection for docility and stable temperament, has produced the modern dog and cat. We cannot expect a few years to do the same to a wild animal. My bottle-raised research wolves, foxes, and coyotes—none of them "pets"—were relatively untrainable compared to various breeds of domestic dog raised in exactly the same way.

Don't think that I'm against wild animals! I'm simply against people owning them as "pets." With few exceptions they end up misfits in man's world. Even when hand-raised from infancy and relatively tame due to socialization, they so often are unpredictable and hard to train. Remember that "tame" and "domesticated" are two different states of being. A wild animal can lose its fear of man, be called tame, and become socialized and attached to its owner; but a domestic animal is at once tame, and socialized and either genetically selected or innately predisposed to fit into man's domestic world. Wild animals are not so preadapted.

No matter how much we try to rationalize and justify keeping wild animals as pets—or keep them in zoos, for that matter—we cannot escape the fact that we deprive them of more than we can ever hope to give in return. Love is not enough for a captive wild spirit. The animal is both a product of and a part of its environment. To remove it from its natural habitat cannot be justified on ethical grounds, except for purposes of education, research, and conservation. Merely to indulge human fancy is unjustifiably selfish and inhumane.

Owning a wild animal helps accelerate their extinction. Thousands of birds, fish, reptiles, monkeys, small wild cats, and other mammals die during their capture or confinement before shipment, or from stress and disease during shipment, long before they reach the pet store.

Some states ban the sale of within-state wild animals—so the stores import stock from the next state! Massachusetts is in the vanguard of working to restrict ownership of any wild animal; not only because of the disease and injury hazards wild animals pose, but for the frequently overstated problem of conservation. Species like margays, ocelots and other of the small spotted South American cats are endangered due to the demand in the United States for their skins (which make such "nice" coats). The public also wants them as pets, thanks to irresponsible advertising, wild-animal programs, and "celebrities" who own such exotic creatures. A pet store in Canada sold a couple of young teenagers two rattlesnakes—how responsible can such stores claim to be? The animals they sell are simply commodities

A red-tailed hawk, one of many species of birds of prey which are kept for the inhumane sport of falconry. Some falconers have helped in conservation, but they unwittingly support a "sport of kings" which is an outdated, selfish, inhumane indulgence.

and setting the price on the cage is their only consideration.

Another problem is posed by falconry. Why must they exploit a wild creature's instinct to kill for the sake of their own pleasure? A hawk kills birds and small rodents in order to live. A falconer has it killed for his own enjoyment—a double exploitation of nature. Add to this the fact that to obtain fledgling hawks, nests are often robbed. It becomes clear that this "sport of kings" is ignoble and selfishly immature in its arrogant shortsightedness.

Rivaling the immorality of falconry is the training and selective breeding of dogs for hunting boar or coyote, or raising bulls to fight a well-armed matador who can always call for back-up support in the bull ring, or breeding dogs and roosters to fight to the death for the enjoyment of the spectators. We indulge ourselves in such cases much too often, forgetting human dignity and the reverence for all life that we as responsible and ethical animals should uphold in our every action. Fortunately, we aren't all like this.

Some animal lovers have backyard bird or raccoon feeders. They probably know enough not to approach a seemingly friendly wild animal in their yard—it might bite and it may have rabies. A rabid animal shows no fear; it may seem, therefore, to be friendly. But beware!

But a well-meant, innocent-seeming bird feeder can be a disaster. One woman I know puts out forty pounds of bird seed each week! Only set out a handful each day. Too much feeding can affect the balance of nature, since overfed birds may produce too many offspring for the area to support. Even worse is the evidence that feeders that attract many birds can become a focal point from which are spread epidemic diseases between birds that normally maintain a safe distance from each other. Thus while an epidemic may have been controlled, the control breaks down if you draw too many birds to the feeder.

Another important point to consider concerns the need of many people to "help" infant wild animals. They find a little fox cub, a fawn, a baby rabbit, or a fledgling bird apparently abandoned by its parents, and take it home to care for. Often the little creature would best be left where you found it; a parent may be hiding from you nearby. Return several hours later just to make sure. An infant bird may be fed by its parents on the ground and thrive, provided that no marauding cats are around. If you are concerned about such a discovery and feel that the animal needs help, think twice if it is not actually imperiled. Then, if you must, call the local humane society, zoo, or state wildlife department for advice.

A tradition inevitably wasteful of animals, a cause of unnecessary suffering to pet and children both, is the presentation of an Easter pet: chicken or duckling or bunny. Mass produced, few survive much longer than the Easter candies and chocolate eggs. Handled excessively by uninstructed children, not properly cared for by uninformed adults, the sad slaughter creates a shadow over a time when we should reflect upon rebirth and renewal.

One of the worst drawbacks to keeping a wild animal as a pet involves other people. Adults and children both often approach a tame wild animal with the same expectations of its behavior as they have of the average pet cat or dog. "It's going to like me if I approach it and talk gently. If it doesn't run away or threaten me it will surely let me pet it." This attitude doesn't always work. Many wild animals don't give warning signals or communicate them like cats and dogs. I often received a hard nip from certain of my foxes because some of their signals were ambiguous. Some tamed animals will allow you to approach to within a certain distance. But unlike a cat or dog, such an animal won't necessarily allow you to pet it—your expectation may be exploded when a beak or tooth sinks into your hand or leg!

Some terrible accidents have occurred in wildlife parks and spots in national forests because people mistakenly think a tame animal acts like a domesticated one. Notorious is the bear: coming too close with a camera, or teasing it too much over a tidbit of food, may provoke aggression. The feeding of wild animals makes them dangerous when they lose their fear of man. Such feeding by the public must be outlawed to protect public and animals alike. Animals that attack or become nuisances often have to be shot.

The moral of this chapter is that you should love wildlife at a distance. If you really do possess a reverence for all life, it goes above and beyond self-interest—do show it, and do what you can to aid your state conservation department, local zoo, or natural-history society.

The care and rearing of wild animals in captivity should be left to experts. They must have state permits; but too many permits are given out—wild-animal ownership should be restricted to research/education/conservation. Anyone with a deep respect for wildlife will think twice before obtaining a creature that must be kept out of its natural context in a cage world, descented, devenomed, declawed, or defanged. Some zoophiles are like stamp collectors, kidding themselves that their private Noah's ark menagerie serves a purpose other than self-gratification or financial gain.

We must all mature to varying degrees—show those on the glamour ego trip of having an exotic wild creature that they must relinquish their ideas and animals; the concerned people who would overfeed, attempt to pet, or otherwise interfere with wild animals and with their habits and ecology must refrain from these actions. Most of us do sincerely care for all creatures great and small—even the misguided sports and trophy hunters and those who train animals to fight and kill for pleasure. We must learn to place the rights of all animals in perspective, and not favor "our" animals for egotistical reasons.

The greatest—perhaps the only—benefit for me in having kept wild animals, apart from the scientific knowledge I gained, is the knowledge that wild animals do not make pets and never will (nor should they). The place for wild animals is in the wilds. The effort expended in trying to keep them as pets would be much better used to work to conserve them in nature where they belong, within the context for which they are naturally adapted.

Today, shortsighted national policies for continued growth (cancerlike "progress"), with the attendant over-

As cuddly as a . . . bear? This little cub immediately evokes a whole set of human emotional responses which might change with the knowledge that it will be of formidable size at two years of age.

exploitation of natural resources, threatens some and destroys other animals and their habitats each day—mining, logging, offshore oil drilling, and so on.

Our children will look back in horror if we do not act now. With the senseless, unfeeling destruction of all that is wild and beautiful, with each irreversible step we become a little more insensitive and callous and a little more inhumane. When an animal dies, or a species becomes extinct, something within us dies also.

Let's bring an end to centuries of man's exploitation of man and nature. Let it be the beginning of a new relationship between man and earth, wherein we discover that in order to be civilized, we need not control, exploit, or destroy the wild and natural things of this world to exhibit our terrible powers of mastery. We must "let it be," and find our own freedom and fulfillment in interacting with all that is wild and free.

Postscript: A Warning

There is a proliferation nationwide of wolf/dog hybrids that are being bred and sold as pets. While they are exotic most of these hybrids are not good pets when they attain maturity. They tend to be shy, emotionally unstable, and sometimes aggressive and unpredictable in their actions toward people (especially strangers) and sometimes toward dogs of the same sex. The breeding and ownership of such animals should be restricted to people engaged in behavioral studies and education. Some few hybrids make good pets; but the majority do not adapt. Breeding and keeping them is *inhumane*. They should be classified as wild animals and subject to state laws controlling wild animals and wild animal ownership. A wildlife owner or breeder's permit should be mandatory and then given only if the animals are kept for behavioral studies or educational purposes, in accordance with the policy of the Humane Society concerning the ownership and breeding of wild animals.

21

Creatures That May Come into Your Life in the Summer

SUMMER VACATIONS CAN produce all kinds of predictable and unpredictable surprises and events. Children and animals in various combinations, like it or not, increase the permutations of the usual diversity of events and experiences at home and on vacation. The unexpected should be expected.

The spring bounty of creation will be hopping, crawling, biting, and, yes, even dying indoors and outdoors, at home and wherever you go for a vacation. Children, perhaps because they explore so many places so thoroughly, come up with all manner of nature's creations. For better or for worse, they bring them home. Or, quite independent of children, you may be invaded by one or more life forms that make you wish summer was over with (if the heat and humidity haven't already).

As an introduction we must consider the following: what to do with animal pests (excluding children); the disposition of wild creatures brought home by the children as "pets" and orphan wild animals they find; and the animals and plants you may find on vacation and want to bring home.

Pests

Last summer an ever-increasing army of wood ants invaded our house. I put the first few outside and asked them not to return—but they did and increased their ranks to hundreds overnight. Jars of preserves and cookies were sealed, but still they came.

I admire ants—they've been around probably a hundred times longer than us hairless apes—and I didn't want to kill them. My wife thought otherwise. They were pests, invaders upon our precious territory, violating our rights to privacy. And some would sting if you accidentally sat on them. So would I if you sat on me! But they didn't come out and sting us, I argued, so why make war? I regularly invaded their territory (the lawns and woods) and without a doubt accidentally crushed them by the dozens. So why kill them because they invaded my neck of the woods? It was not as if they had singled us out for personal reasons.

In the end I didn't war upon them. There was no pressing reason to: they don't carry diseases that could harm us, and we weren't concerned that our houseguests would think us odd or unsanitary hicks in allowing a colony of ants to cohabit with us. We don't invite houseguests who think like that. ("Only ants," did you say?)

One day the ants were gone. Just like that. I guessed they had taken enough provisions to set up their city outdoors. Since summer was just beginning, they could live off the land for the rest of the season.

No need to put bug spray down—and so add to the vast quantities of cancer- and birth-defect-creating chemicals already in our air, food, water, and bodies. No need to crush them in the final declaration of all-out war—a hopeless task anyway, considering their numbers—and then have to cope with guilt. After all, they want to live as much as you or I. Socially speaking, they are our kin.

What should you do with other household invaders— wasps, bees, hornets, outdoor spiders, June bugs, and the like? Squash them before they get you? That is a really fine

If you find a wild animal, study it, but don't keep it. It's not yours to keep. *(John Dommers, HSUS)*

Encouraging wild animals to your door could mean trouble for you or them. *(Helen West, HSUS)*

example for the kids! Don't play into your paranoia. These
creatures aren't out to get you. They are *scared*. If you'll
look at them, you'll see that they only want out. Why not
help them? A piece of cardboard slipped under a cup is a
quick, safe trap—then you can transport the insects intact
and deposit them outdoors. You will become an example of
humane compassion and ecological awareness for your
children!

There are other summer pests that require a firmer
hand—warfare if you wish. But let's try detente and then
deterrents first. I'm not talking of a deterrent like one of
those outdoor lights which attracts night bugs and fries
them with an electric arc current. People who have these
devices should be covered with honey and tied to the
ground in the Amazon jungle for an hour. Half an hour
would do. These obscene offspring of consumer technology
indiscriminately destroy useful and beautiful and harmless
"bugs"—moths, preying mantises, fireflies, and other insects—by the billions. Why? So the cocktail hour on the
patio will be bug-free?

Summer *is* bugs. Why should we kill all bugs because a
few bite? You can avoid going out at sunset when the mosquitoes, midges, gnats, and "no see 'ums" are out in force.
Lemon oil or some other insect repellent applied to yourself
is fair and ecologically sensible warfare. A smoke bomb in
your yard will drive you away temporarily; a chemical
bomb may give you cancer twenty summers hence. Ultrasonic devices to drive away mosquitoes are commercially
available and they do work. Such a device, personal insect
repellent, or mosquito netting (especially!) are fair play.
Chemical warfare, or draining or spreading oil on lakes and
ditches, is insane. Destroy all the bugs and you'll probably
do the rest of the world in, including yourself!

Some unwelcome parasites multiply in the house during
the summer. These include fleas, ticks, and brown recluse
spiders. Fumigation by your local pest-control agent is essential to keep them down and, to be effective, may have to
be repeated at monthly intervals. I'm sure you will want to
live and let live if you have house martens or other birds

nesting under the eaves of your house. But bats in your belfry (or attic) may cause you some anxiety, since they can carry rabies virus. Personally, I would rather have a series of painless rabies inoculations and let my home be their safe haven. But that would be my own choice and I would carry the personal responsibility. Don't forget to consider that the shots required *after* being bitten by a rabid animal are far from painless!

Part of your home territory is your garden. If you do grow flowers, fruit trees, and vegetables, I recommend getting some books on natural methods of pest control. Many pesticides are carcinogens, and many cancers are caused by such environmental agents. One in four of us will die from cancer over the next decade, and there's nothing to indicate that we have cancer under control.

And please be careful with what insecticides, herbicides (weed killers), and disinfectants you do use in and outside your home in the summer. Insect sprays and vapona strips can make your pet sick—parakeets and cats are especially susceptible.

Good screens on doors and windows to keep bugs out and sticky flypaper and a flyswatter inside are all you need. If possible, keep porch lights off so you won't attract too many bugs to the house at night. A yard light will draw them harmlessly away. Don't encourage your pet to hunt bugs with you—it might suffer a bee or wasp sting.

Bug-killing DDT, chlorodane, lindane, malathion, and other insecticides pose special dangers to cats; spraying around the house and in their litter tray with Lysol or any other coal-tar phenol derivative also can sicken them. So keep Lysol away from cats when musty house and animal smells appear in the summer. (Baking soda is a good litter tray deodorant for those hot and humid summer days.) If you must use deodorant/disinfectant, use a safe one containing chlorophyll or a natural perfume such as lemon oil.

If you have a large lawn, say an acre or more in size, please don't apply worm killer. Earth containing no worms is dead earth.

Why not allow a section of lawn to grow wild as a meadow? Neighbors may complain—but it is your legal right to allow any part of your property to go wild. Many useful and/or beautiful insects and other creatures—butterflies, harmless lizards, turtles, snakes—are endangered. You could provide them with a haven. Your small meadow will also attract interesting birds and wildlife. Too many natural meadows across the country are being destroyed—to be replaced with parking lots, housing developments, airports, highways, and factories. We can do our small bit to help preserve the wild spaces.

Children's "Finds"

Children will come home with various "finds." Caterpillars, frog spawn and tadpoles (pollywogs), snakes, mice, baby rabbits and birds, lightning bugs, fish, butterflies—you name it, they find it.

There are several rules to be followed.

First rule. Poking unsupervised under stones and bushes could mean trouble—scorpions, in some areas; snakes, in many. Discourage this behavior. Children should know how to recognize venomous creatures; and you should be able to teach them!

Second rule. Anything collected is to be returned *alive.* What is collected should be kept safely and held under conditions as near natural as possible. A vivarium glass tank with moist moss, ferns, and rocks is fine for toads, salamanders, turtles, snakes, and lizards; add dry sand and rock "cover" if they are desert species. Such creatures should be released where they were first collected after a day or two. A glass jar, sealed with perforated top, containing a little moist cotton or soil and a few sprigs of natural food, the vegetation from which they were collected, is right for keeping bugs and caterpillars. A clean jar or tank of pond or river water, along with a little water-weed, will suffice for most aquatic creatures.

Because few wild creatures will eat in captivity, even if

With patience and experience, the rewards of helping wildlife, especially orphaned creatures, are many.

(R.F. Rodriguez, HSUS)

ildren can learn some of the
hest humane values from being
osed to their animal kin early in
. Curiosity can lead to under-
nding, and affection to responsi-
compassion for all life.

(Art Ketchum, HSUS)

they can be given the proper foods, they should only be kept for a maximum forty-eight-hour observation period. Exceptions are caterpillars, frog spawn, and tadpoles; they can be released when they have matured somewhat or metamorphosed, and usually pose no problems as far as eating in captivity is concerned.

Don't encourage your children to collect frogs, snakes, salamanders, and the like for scientific supply houses. The negative ecological consequences and the unethical nature of such collecting greatly outweigh the small amount the children may earn from such ventures. In addition, children combing through an area may do much inadvertent damage to vegetation and unseen creatures. (This is why it is important to stay *on* the trails and footpaths in national and state parks.)

Third rule. If an "orphan" wild animal is found—a healthy baby skunk, raccoon, possum, rabbit, or fawn—leave it where you came upon it. Its mother may well be nearby. If obvious danger threatens it, if it is beside a busy roadside or is being chased by dogs or is injured, that's a different matter entirely. In such cases move it out of danger. Take it home only as a last resort. Then call your local humane shelter or regional division of the state wildlife or fish and game department. The same rule holds for nest-fallen fledgling birds. Avoid handling any wild creature you find—your odor may disturb its parents and cause them to reject it. It might also be rabid; a bite from a rabid fox cub or skunk could mean more than a premature end to an otherwise happy summer!

Fourth rule. Plants. Few people give collecting bunches of wild flowers a second thought, even digging up pretty ones—wild orchids, ferns, cacti, and other popular varieties. Overzealous, indiscriminate collecting is to be avoided. Dozens of plant species are endangered today because of summer collectors. Some states—Arizona is one—will stop and search your vehicle at the border to protect their plant life. That day on the hillside or in the forest you may have been alone—but thousands of visitors during that season, and then across several seasons, have an unrelenting impact. So—if you *must*—take only one of the most common plants for your herbarium or wild garden or meadow.

Be sure to avoid importation of out-of-state (nonindigenous) plants and living creatures. Importation of foreign plants (and wild animals) is not permitted by law.

Fifth rule. Don't pick up wildlife from river, lake, seashore, forest, or desert during vacation, either accidentally or intentionally. It's always a good idea to sweep out your camper and shake out sleeping bags and tents to prevent unintentional visitors. Do resist purposely taking a nonindigenous animal—bug or beast—back home. You would not be able to follow the second rule, releasing it where you found it, after keeping it for a few days' enjoyment and observation. And accidental infestation is an added risk to consider.

Help foster youthful interest in wildlife on vacation by purchasing wildlife and plant guidebooks—identification is fun; imparting and storing knowledge probably will stimulate your own curiosity. Lenses and binoculars are useful, too, and a camera can furnish pictures to take back with you—instead of perishable living things.

Avoid the temptation of buying a hermit crab inside its shell and other wild creatures often sold at resort-area stores and airports. And if you go to Alaska or Canada don't get hooked into buying wild-animal products—wild furs (seal, wolf) and carved walrus ivory and other such items. You are only supporting a system of needless and often painful killing of wild creatures. Shark jaws, puffer fish, and similar seashore trophies offered for sale in resort towns should be avoided, too. If you can't find your own on the beach as a result of natural deaths, please think twice about supporting this small industry—the senseless killing of animals for the small profits derived from the sale of knickknack trophies and souvenirs will continue as long as there is a demand.

In spite of all these cautions, I really do wish you have a good summer. Mother Nature certainly will continue to provide her share if you keep in mind what I have said and see to it that your children are well informed, too.

P.S. If children really want some animal/plant/nature contact this summer, remember there are excellent nature-study summer camps, local natural-history and Audubon Society programs, and, for older children, part-time jobs at humane shelters, veterinary hospitals, zoos, and wildlife refuges and parks. The Humane Society of the United States, 2100 L. Street NW, Washington, D.C. 20037, publishes several useful pamphlets on the care of wild creatures and careers with animals; also *KIND* magazine for children. The more they read and learn, the more they will enjoy the precious heritage of the outdoors and of our animal kin—beasts, bugs, and all!

22

The Use and Abuse
of Animals in Zoos

I AM A child again, sitting next to my parents on the bus
home after a visit to the zoo. My feet are tired, my hands
sticky with candy floss, and my mind is mulling over the
day as I gaze out of the window. It was a big zoo and I got
weary but I was too old to ask to be carried. The best things
were petting that baby elephant and riding on a camel. It
was a pity the waiting line for the zoo train was too long.
How incredibly big were the elephants and rhinos and they
smelled like pigs and horses all mixed up. The gorilla
smelled like Daddy after he had worked in the garden but
all those monkeys confused me. They would play and fight
and scream and do funny things that I'm not supposed to
do. I don't understand them. Worst were the lions and tigers and wolves. They were all asleep and were boring.
Someone tried to wake up the lion by throwing pennies at
him and someone else disobeyed the rules by banging on
the glass of some other animals that were asleep. They
seemed bored too. I felt sorry for them. They had nothing
to play with either. A polecat made me dizzy by running in
circles all the time. Daddy said he was crazy. I held a guinea pig and stroked a baby llama in the children's zoo but
there were too many kids. I like to be alone when I talk to

animals. The giraffe reminded me of my cousin who's grown up all of a sudden and won't play or even look at me anymore. The reptile house was creepy and I got bored with all those sleeping snakes and the birdhouse was full of noises and colors. One of the parrots spoke to me there but the others didn't seem to see me. It will be good to get home and run in the fields with my dog Gruff. Hope he won't chase the cows again. I'm sleepy. I don't want to be a lion tamer anymore, or a keeper like the one in charge of the chimp's tea party. They looked silly, all dressed up and making a mess. When I grow up I'm going to let all the animals out of their cages, except the lions, gorillas, and alligators. And I'll have an elephant and a cheetah or a tiger as a pet. Like Sabu, the jungle boy.

It's easy to recall these childhood memories because zoos haven't changed much in the last thirty years. Even new ones still build the old Victorian type iron-bar prisons, now updated with hygienic ceramic tiles and automatic water flushes for the floors. Admittedly, some zoos are designing more open, barless enclosures with retaining moats, but the apparent openness is often an illusion since the animals do not, in fact, have more space. Also, some animals do fall into the moats and drown or injure themselves. After a storm flooded a moat at one zoo, the bears were able to swim out and have a few hours of freedom before being caught. But is cage space the only requirement for wild animals in captivity?

Twenty years ago, the sight of a panther pacing neurotically in its iron cage in a zoo in Paris left me with an indelible memory. Each time it circled its cage, it rubbed its right side against the bars and the entire flank had become a massive suppurating ulcer.

A few years later, a visit to the open park zoo at Whipsnade in England and more recently to a safari-type zoo in California gave me a little optimism. The evidence of overgrazing and destruction of trees was an obvious ecological problem to be solved, but the animals looked better and, more important still, they were *doing* something. They

A clean and barren zoo prison. Fortunately, some zoos are now
making improvements.

were not all sleeping or pacing neurotically but were behaving, communicating, and interacting. They were alive and so different from the semianimate, vegetating zoo captives that were as reactive as the glassy-eyed, stuffed museum specimens.

While many zoos are merely collections, interestingly the main research focus of most zoo veterinary hospitals is on pathology. Regrettably, research on behavior, social needs, and group dynamics has been minimal, and of course no ecological studies are even contemplated. When the entire world of the animal is a ten-foot by ten-foot cage, the environment does affect behavior and the two interact and influence susceptibility to disease. Attempts to make the barren cage one-tenth of one per cent more "natural" by adding a sand pit, a rope, or a dead tree branch and further experimenting to improve this microenvironment are few and far between. What can be done and what is being done to alleviate this deplorable and depressing situation? Is the old-style zoo to be done away with, as some would have, or can some improvements be made? How about the attitudes of those who manage zoos—are they as inflexible, conceptually, as the cages are architecturally? The Humane Society of the United States claims, "As long as there is one animal caged without an educational purpose, the Humane Society and all humanitarians have work to do."

Traditionally, zoos have been for the curious who, from the Middle Ages in Europe, gazed in awe at the enormousness of the elephant, the grace of the gazelle, the power of the lion, and saw something of themselves in gorilla and chimpanzee. Adults and children alike got a feeling for the incredible diversity of life and of the many diverging and converging paths that various species have taken in their evolution. This was educational and even today most zoos provide little more than this, additions being (sometimes) a map of the animal's range and list of food and habits in the wild beneath its common and Latin names. The more animals in the "stamp collection," the more prestige that zoo had over others. Additional "attractions" might include a chimp or lion show, which gave the public no further insights about the behavior and social lives of the animals. A circus within a zoo is no improvement.

The collection mania led to the ludicrous position where one zoo might exhibit a single specimen and make no attempt to trade it or give it to another zoo that had one of the same species of the opposite sex. So much for conservation. Worse still, gregarious species housed alone suffered the consequences of social deprivation. Until recently, zoos were often unaware of what their neighboring zoos had in their collection and only surplus stock for trade were advertised. Now communication between zoos is improving since the establishment of the Association of Zoological Gardens and Aquariums. Past records, however, of sources of origin (where and when caught or from what zoo a given animal was acquired) have been inadequate. Such information, for example, is essential for research and conservation of many subspecies of primate and wolf.

Many zoos have been forced to improve their animal facilities by the 1970 Animal Welfare Act. Improved nutrition, sanitation, increased cage size and lessened crowding are only part of what is needed. The entire concept of zoos has to be radically changed, first in terms of the environment—cage size is only one aspect; complexity in terms of play objects, manipulanda, ledges, bridges, and tunnels to create spatial complexity and variability must be studied. Second is the animal itself. Permanent or seasonal need for companionship, optimal group size, sex and age ratios, and group dynamics have to be explored. In some species, inadequate social stimulation can interfere with reproduction. Crowding stress can cause infertility, greater aggression, and susceptibility to disease. Inadequate housing can disrupt maternal behavior so that offspring are ignored or even cannibalized. Boredom in an empty cage not only causes neurotic, stereotyped pacing and circling, but also a hypertrophy of intensification of normal behaviors. For example, grooming may increase and lead to further feather- or hairpulling and ultimately to self-mutilation and autophagia. Toes and tails are eaten; in one zoo a bear began to groom its abdomen and finally eviscerated itself. Without a partner or work to do (such as searching for food and prey killing) sexual and prey-killing behaviors may be redirected toward an inanimate object, such as a food bowl. The animal's tail may become a substitute prey to chase and its own abdomen a sexual substitute.

When given a larger cage, a long-caged animal may not use the additional space. A bear, kept for years in a circus trailer cage, paced for weeks in an oblong stereotyped pattern the same dimensions as its cage when placed in a large zoo enclosure. The need for space is not the only problem; companionship and environmental complexity to prevent the development of neurotic compulsions are needed.

Often when an animal has been caged alone for a long time it will not allow another into its territory; it may even kill it. Gorillas and chimps whose mothers refuse to care for them are usually raised in the children's zoo. In this way they often become imprinted onto people and not their own kind. As they get older and harder to handle they are put into the ape house. Like many animals that die of depression when a mate dies, so these young humanized animals become depressed when placed with their own kind. Missing human contact, they may die, or simply withdraw and never become integrated with their own species-group. This also affects conservation, since they will often not breed. Imagine zoos of the future having to hand-rear and artificially inseminate most of their stock. In one zoo, a hand-raised (and therefore humanized) bull moose, when first introduced to female moose, tried to mount its keeper! In another zoo, a pair of very rare bongos were on exhibit. Both had been hand-raised and had no prior experience with each other and when put together for the first time showed little interest. They have never shown any signs of breeding. A mature, hand-raised gorilla was at last found a mate in another zoo. When the female was put in his cage, he immediately tore off her arm and killed her. He, and other humanized animals, with inadequate socialization earlier in life with their own kind, are the psychologically sterile specimens doomed for a life of solitary confinement.

Clearly, much behavior research is needed to improve the mental health of animals in zoos and also to insure that they will breed and raise healthy offspring because increasing numbers of animals are now extinct or endangered in the wild. Such knowledge could also be used to beef up educational programs. A pictorial chart of the various displays and communication signals of various species would be the first step.

Few question why a lion or buffalo has a mane, a wild ram a hairy and pendulous dewlap or chest, a Brahmin bull a hump on his shoulders. These are all fake enlargements—like padded shoulders—to give an illusion of great size and are important therefore as display structures. In juvenile males they are poorly developed. It is not only such odd shapes and structures that are important behaviorally, but also colors. The thin, dark semicircle under the eyes of many animals, such as coyotes and gazelles, serves the same function as in a football player, namely to stop sunlight from bouncing off the cheekbones into the eyes. The white tip on the tail of a fox enhances tail movements that are important social signals. The bright colors of many birds often serves the same function as singing—namely to attract or "advertise" for females and to display occupancy of territory to rival males. Females are dowdy and unimpressive usually because it is they who must wear camouflage so they will be well concealed while on the nest. Many species of tropical fish have bright colors that similarly serve as territorial "flags" but some species change color when they are afraid, submissive, ready to fight, breed, or are taking care of young—a whole language of colors! Some animals, such as poisonous snakes and insects, have bright red and yellow or black and yellow aposematic or warning colors—they advertise the fact that they are dangerous.

Few zoos inform the public that when rival male snakes fight, they simply wrestle and push until one is exhausted and submits. They do not use their venom on each other—the fighting is ritualized and has its own built-in laws. Similarly, mammals with massive horns like the oryx never use their weapons against each other; rival males simply have a push-of-war and only use their lancelike horns to defend themselves from lions. Giraffes have tiny horns that are used in ritual combat but they are far from helpless. Their front hooves can smash a lion's skull.

An informative booklet could be printed by every zoo, providing brief notations of the behavioral significance of such structural peculiarities in animals, and the public would be enriched with an appreciation of the anatomy of behavior. As it is in many zoos today, there is virtually little else to see or learn, and such information would help justify keeping animals. Without such knowledge, people leave the zoo, unimpressed, confused, and often amused at the great diversity, shape, size, and color of the animal world. Zoos must inform, not titillate and entertain with "rare," "dangerous," "cute," and circuslike performing animals, or seek to impress by the size and diversity of their "collection." Diversity in nature has evolutionary significance, as has similarity in convergence in structure and function. At one level it is entertaining, at another it is informative. With such knowledge, a deeper understanding and respect for life might be perpetrated (which is much needed) for the benefit of man and fellow animals alike.

A while back I gave a workshop on behavior disorders in zoo animals to some two-hundred or more members of the American Association of Zoo Veterinarians. Their concern and interest has given me much optimism. They are now aware of the fact that diseases and injuries make up only a small proportion of the problems that they have to face, and indeed that behavioral and disease problems are often interrelated. The next question is what to do; phase out old urban zoos and develop suburban safari parks, or simply, development of the latter, leaving the urban zoo to be the center for intensive research and propagation of endangered species which, when established, could be moved out to the safari park. Surplus young born in the park could be used to stock the children's zoo. I for one believe that contact areas, where children can touch and experience directly, are educationally valid; they are also usually the most popular part of the zoo. Zoo management must balance unnecessary propagation of wild animals in captivity with the need to maintain and conserve genetically viable stock.

As emphasized earlier, the more we learn about a particular animal's needs and behavior, the more we can enhance its care and propagation; we will also have more educational material to provide for the public. The fee-operated tape recorder in front of some exhibits in a few zoos today is a beginning. In some zoos they have unfortunately replaced all guided educational tours, while others still provide such tours at a moment's notice for small groups. More curators today are young college graduates who are articulate and have the necessary biological background for clearly and objectively describing behavior and giving pertinent information. Many begin as keepers and work their way up; the job is interesting and is gaining respect, at last. Zoos are looking now for educated and responsible young people rather than employing semiliterates and ex-farmhands who prefer city life and will work for dimes scooping poop. Admittedly, a few of these old-timers really love their animals and after years of experience have a wealth of information; but nothing has been recorded or systematically described by them and consequently much is lost. Educational programs for keepers, encouragement to attend local college classes and write up experiences for publication in the *International Zoo Year Book* are the beginnings of a constructive career program.

Keepers and curators in a few zoos, Brookfield (near Chicago) for one, run weekend high-school projects at the zoo. Direct and continuing contact this way, over several weeks, is a fine learning experience for many students. In addition, some zoos reach a wider local audience with a weekly or monthly TV show. Often the content of these programs leaves much to be desired, but the beginning is promising. Marlin Perkins's national network *Wild King-dom* grew out of his TV zoo show in St. Louis.

The prognosis for city zoos is good in the long but not in the short term. Many are lacking funds even to provide adequate housing; others have to take time phasing out old personnel who can't simply be sacked and replaced by younger, better-educated recruits. A few zoos are stuck with new cages designed in the traditional prison manner and are having difficulty in justifying additional funds for housing.

Zoos are needed. They provide an important link with "nature" for urban man, whose life-style increasingly isolates and alienates him from nature. The safari-type zoo is obviously more "natural" for man and beast alike. Zoos in many cities give knowledge and pleasure to millions of children, but without improving the housing and care of the animals, no educational program, no matter how informative and innovative, can be justified.

Zoos also have a vital role to play in conservation of many endangered species. They are becoming the "gene banks" of many species that will be extinct in the wild before man can restore the ecocidal imbalances caused by overpopulation, pollution, and overexploitation of the biosphere.

Zoos not only need financial support but an infusion of innovative inquiry and applied research. For example, some are experimenting with mixed exhibits—goats and monkeys together or zebras, camels, and giraffes. Placing different species together that normally cohabit in the wild is a relatively recent idea; we see more behavior and the environment is more enriched in this way for and by the animals themselves. Nocturnal mammals, for years exhibited as sleeping mummies in broad daylight, can now be found alive and active in "night rooms" with sufficient red light for people to see them, but not enough to make them think it is daylight. When it is night, bright lights are turned on and they all go to sleep.

Many of the techniques and equipment used by animal psychologists on laboratory animals could also be applied to zoo animals. Several years ago, Dr. Hediger, a well-known European zoo director, emphasized that zoo animals should be given work to do. They would be trained, not to perform for the public as in a circus, but rather to prevent boredom and behavioral degeneration in an otherwise unstimulating and unvarying environment. Most animals, birds, zebras, lions and apes, and even reptiles, could be given an operant device, such as a disk or bar to press in order to get food. This can be made quite complex by training the animal only to press the bar when a light or buzzer goes on, and the bar has to be pressed five or ten times before food is dispensed. Other things can be done besides providing rubber tires and ropes for monkeys and apes to swing and climb. They like to make nests out of hay—but that makes the cage look too untidy. They can be taught to put up ladders, stack boxes, and slot fishing poles together to reach food. They will press a bar in order to see slides or movies, too, and can be taught not only to fingerpaint (all royalties to the zoo!) but to solve puzzles. Puzzle tests, such as having to choose a red cube from a heap of different colored ones, or a triangle-shaped one in preference to a cube or a hexagon, can be given. This is not only good for the animal but is also entertaining and informative for the public.

Dr. Keller Breland has a unique zoo, the "I.Q. Zoo," in Hot Springs, Arkansas, where he employs operant (Skinnerian) conditioning in his animal exhibits. Raccoons play basketball, hens play baseball, a duck beats a drum, pigs clean up a cluttered room, a goat dances, and macaws race on roller skates. These are a little circuslike, but other exhibits demonstrate chimp intelligence, the strength of a bear, and the accuracy with which a squirrel can leap. These latter exhibits, demonstrating the natural abilities of an animal, are what is needed now in other zoo "museums." The animals are active, working, and at the same time educating the public.

Some psychologists have taught chimps not only to use "coins" of different denomination in a slot machine food dispenser, but to communicate in deaf-and-dumb sign language and to "write" with symbols. Of course all this takes time and money, but a few animals kept this way would be better than many, left to rot with nothing to interest them and therefore being of little or no interest to the public.

Much can be done with nonprimates too, especially with social groups of mice, goats, and wolves, for example. A simple chart showing what to look out for—dominance displays, sexual and maternal behavior, relations between adults and infants and communication signals—should be available. Closed-circuit TV (designed for lowlight levels) has potential too, especially for showing within-den behavior as when she-wolf or bear is giving birth and later nursing her cubs.

"Feeding time" for the big cats is usually posted, and this is often the only time they behave. At least some of the smaller carnivores could be given live prey, such as live crickets to catch, this being another therapeutic work activity; but giving them mice or rats might offend certain visitors. The fishing cats at Brookfield Zoo are given a few fish in a "stream" in their cage each day to catch. This is one of the most popular exhibits now. More thought along such lines could greatly enhance the usefulness of zoos, not as museums but as places to learn something about animal behavior. Unhappy and understimulated animals do not behave.

If people are not given any information, they fill in the void with fantasies and project and hand on such misinformation to their children. "Yes, wolves are savage and would eat you up, son." The only comments while looking at a gorilla are invariably, "Wow, he looks like he could kill anything"; "Look at those mean eyes!" Animals are categorized as dumb, stupid, clumsy, comical, agile, swift, cruel, savage, powerful, wise, cunning, dangerous, ruthless, and so on. All are anthropomorphic projections, helped little by fairy tales and fables and pronouncements by uninterested or ill-informed parents and teachers.

A classic example of misinterpretation, even by experts,

concerns the alleged hypersexuality of monkeys like the rhesus and baboon. Embarrassed adults distract the children to something else or give a half answer when they see monkey after monkey mounting and thrusting. A sex orgy seems to be going on. Far from the truth. Most of what is seen is not sexual, but social dominance. Male or female mounts another male or female to assert rank over it and a low-ranking male or female presents itself to be mounted as a signal of submission. Also, all the grooming that monkeys do is not to pick lice and fleas off each other. It is simply a friendly, contact-maintaining activity which binds friendships and helps make things up after an argument. Admittedly they may groom more when there is nothing else to do, and more fighting and pseudo-sexual mounting will occur with overcrowding, but these two examples serve to show how easy it is to misperceive what is actually going on.

Zoos, like so many things in our society, are being scrutinized as our values, needs, and perceptions of the world around us have changed. We are beginning to see what catastrophic ramifications our ignorance, bad habits and complacency are having on the biosphere. The age of Aquarius is upon us, and like a child who has in a previous age pulled the tops off all the flowers in the garden, we are now trying to save what precious animals we can. Attitudes and values have changed; the resources of the world are not infinite; each flower counts now and we must cherish, nurture and restore what is left. A New York cab driver summed this up well for me—"The less people care about nature and all that, the less they care about each other."

I see a greater care and concern dawning now for our zoo animals after years of complacency, apathy, ignorance, and infantile collecting of animals, like stamps. There is much to be done, to be learned and tested and I hope you will make your next visit to the zoo something more than an afternoon outing to keep the kids occupied before dinner!

I "interviewed" my six-year-old son after completing this chapter, to get his impressions about zoos. First, I was

astounded by how much he knew, but he said two very relevant things, with no prompting from me. He would "like
movies or something at the zoo to learn more about how
they behave and do things." Also, "animals in zoos aren't
happy. They need beds and I would give them lots of fruit
and good food and six balls to play with. They need company. I would stay with them on Sunday nights. I could take
them on walks in the country and teach them not to attack
and let them all go free. Elephants would pick up bad people and take them out."

23

Animal Goods That Are No Good

A FRIEND OF mine who recently returned from a vacation in Kashmir was greatly annoyed by U.S. customs officials. Among his purchases—which included two beautiful genuine Kashmir rugs (to his chagrin he later learned that they were machine-made and not worth the hand-made price he had paid)—was a leopard-skin jacket for his wife. He was not allowed to bring it into the country, since federal regulations now ban the importation of *any* products—skins, coats, hats, and the like—from *any* spotted wild cat. This category includes South American ocelots, margays, jaguars, and, of course, African and Asiatic cheetahs and leopards. Why? Because they are all endangered species. Let us hope that this regulation stopping such importation will help save these animals from extinction; other rules, if enforced, might save other types of animals.

"But it was already dead when I bought it, so what's the loss?" Such a common excuse and rationalization. Buying any such products only ensures that more animals will be killed.

Many people in the fur business and exotic-animal-products trade claim that the hunters and trappers do not overkill. They say it would be against their interests to destroy too many animals since that would mean the end of their (bloody) business. But this is far from the truth. Native hunters and trappers will kill animals into extinction for a few dollars per pelt. The harder an animal is to get, the more its pelt is worth; the more the pelt is worth the more intense will be the efforts to obtain the animals to fulfill the market demand.

To counter this catastrophic trend in the United States, several furbearing animals have been put on the Endangered Species List for this country. The wolf, for example, is supposedly fully protected; no one may sell a wolf pelt trapped or shot in the United States. However, since the demand for wild furs persists, trappers and hunters now focus their efforts on furbearers not on the endangered list. Unprotected animals such as lynx, fox, and bobcat suffer the consequences.

How is one to know, especially when visiting a foreign country, what purchases would be subject to federal wildlife laws and the prohibition against importation of various products of endangered species? The government has pamphlets on the subject, and I will describe some of these products. A safe rule of thumb is to avoid buying *anything* made from any animal that is not domesticated. Importation of crocodile and alligator materials—shoes, handbags, wallets, belts, luggage, and other products—is prohibited. So, as a consequence, many stores seek to fulfill the market demand with snakeskin products, saying in justification: "There are plenty of snakes. They aren't on the protected list." Don't listen to such arguments. Soon snakes *will* be endangered and protected, and some species will be extinct before they are protected by law.

Don't buy any wild-animal product, whether it is federally permissible to import it or not.

It's easy to get caught, though, not realizing that some beautifully handcrafted product comes from a wild animal. Scrimshaw etching on whalebone or walrus ivory, or figurines, curios, pendants, and jewelry crafted from the same materials seem far removed from anything alive. But federal laws prohibit the importation of any whale or walrus products. And that prohibition goes for sealskins and seal

The thought of killing a wild animal for fun, for its fur, or any other reason becomes unthinkable when one comes to know and respect it, be it a wolf or any wild creature. *(Scott Barry)*

products, too—in the form of coats, jackets, sealskin toys, purses, wallets or key cases! Any products from polar bear, sea otter, manatees, and dugongs (sea cows) are banned also.

A few summers ago I had a long talk with an Eskimo hunter in Point Barrow, Alaska. His crew, in a tiny boat, had just killed the fourteenth whale that summer for their village. They would celebrate that night.

He sold me two pieces of baleen—the twelve-foot-long horn and hair food filters from the creature's mouth—the tourist's trophy from Alaska analogous to the tusks of an African elephant (except that Eskimos don't kill whales for tourists or poach upon them for the profiteers). After the sale, I asked him about the proposed international regulations to control the slaughter of whales. Many species now verge upon extinction, thanks to the large Japanese and Russian floating factory ships that in a single trip process dozens of whales lured by "hunter" ships. As far as he was concerned, no international regulations could take away the native right to hunt; so much of their cultural traditions and their very tribal identity hinge upon such a way of life. Compared to the commercial concerns, the dent native hunting made on such endangered species was minimal anyway.

A few days later I bought a sealskin at the local trading post; because the seal had been killed by a native hunter, I told myself it was all right. My Eskimo hunter friend and his companions ate all of the whale they had killed. But what of the creature formerly inside the skin I had bought? Not long after I had carefully cut the sealskin up and sewn it into a beautiful vest, I saw through my own rationalization: I was helping create a market for the native hunter, subverting his culture, encouraging him to kill for profit— normally he would kill only a few animals each year to supply the immediate needs of his community. I haven't worn my fine vest since then, and former-president Ford's controversial wolf-skin coat is now apparently in mothballs.

Native hunting, as part of the economy of village life, is ecologically and ethically acceptable. But once it becomes commercialized, either as a local tourist industry or as an export business (like the until-recent exportation of tiger skins from India), then it becomes ecologically unsound and ethically untenable.

But when you are among the local people, who are wearing sealskin parkas, or carved beads of elephant ivory, or fur hats and jackets of leopard or ocelot, it is easy to be tempted to buy their attractive wares. So too is their art tempting—exquisitely carved walrus or elephant ivory, silver-inlaid tiger claws, sea-turtle "tortoiseshell" jewelry. But consider that the trimmings on native masks, headgear, and coats may come from rare and endangered reptiles, birds, and mammals.

In the Cayman Isles, West Indies, there is a commercial sea-turtle ranch where one can buy tortoiseshell jewelry without infringing upon the law. Actually most of their turtles come from eggs taken in the wild; this commercial venture is—at least at its present stage of development—ecologically and ethically questionable.

So too would I question the native exploitation of other animal artifacts, ranging from dried inflated puffer fish to taxidermic obscenities like a mongoose fighting a snake or a bullfrog playing a piano. Few people would ever, in their right minds, purchase such junk—but from Bombay to Acapulco, such artifacts are a common sight in tourist shops, and wrongheaded impulse buying must be avoided.

Over four-hundred species of animals are officially on the endangered list. They must not be imported live, as parts of manufactured items or as hunting trophies. Exceptions may be granted by federal permit for limited scientific or breeding purposes.

The following quotation from a U.S. Fish and Wildlife Service pamphlet clearly summarizes the official government position regarding the purchase and importation of items you might think innocuous:

> Some of the most beautiful and interesting souvenirs that are for sale to travelers are made from the furs, hides, shells, feathers, teeth, and flesh of animals threatened with extinction. Although such souvenirs can be bought legally in many foreign countries, Federal law makes it illegal to import them into the United States, which has pledged its support for the conservation of threatened and endangered animals worldwide.
>
> Should you consider purchasing a wildlife product during your travels, first make sure that you can legally bring it home. And don't be fooled by the argument that the "animal is already dead so it makes no difference if you buy a product made from it." If you should purchase items made from protected animals, you, the consumer, would be adding to the demand for these products and supporting the market for which more animals will be killed.

If you have any questions, contact your local branch of the Fish and Wildlife Service.

As for buying or selling wildlife and wildlife products within the United States, there are also federal laws which restrict interstate commerce involving migratory birds, bald or golden eagles, endangered species, and any wildlife that is taken, transported, possessed, or sold illegally in any state or country. Look out, then, for stuffed preparations or any jewelry or curious or native (Indian) artifacts made from the fur or feathers of any creature.

Let us not simply adhere to regulations and federal laws—rather let our actions be determined by a strong ethical principle of reverence for all life. That means not buying any artifact, no matter how valuable, rare, or appealing, that comes from any wild animal, common or endangered.

24

Animal Abuse and Misuse

SANE AND SENSIBLE animal lovers often become incensed when they hear or see of someone pampering a pooch with clothes, nail polish, hair tint, and other extreme indulgences. Some people seem to go overboard in treating their pets, even to the extent of dressing them up like children. The sane and sensible critics claim that it's abnormal and cruel to make a dog live like that. This common conclusion I cannot support, unless the overindulgence (as with an improper diet) is actually detrimental to the pet's health. If a lonely person chooses to pamper an already dependent pet and finds emotional satisfaction in so doing, there is surely more good than harm in such a relationship.

Other purists deplore the neutering and declawing of dogs and cats, maintaining that it is cruel to deny any animal the right to live as natural a life as possible. In fact, neutering and declawing pets often make them more adaptable to—and so happier in—the confines and privations of modern living.

But there are many ways in which animals, both wild and tame, are really abused and misused today. I want to draw attention to some of the ways so that you may begin to understand how widespread is the misuse and abuse of animals. There is a very fine line between the enjoyment and use of animals and their exploitation and abuse. Understanding can be the first step toward responsible action, and lead ultimately to social change.

Our attitudes and actions toward animals need radical revision, because in general animals are still considered part of our natural "resources." The utilitarian principle—that animals are for man's exclusive use (since he has dominion over them)—is ethically and ecologically untenable; informed people understand that much as the heliocentric theory of the universe showed man the earth was not the center of the universe, so the humanocentive view of the world must be changed to a respect for all life.

One of the worst abuses of pets today is their commercial mass production on the puppy-mill farms that supply large pet-store chains. I have visited such puppy farms and can attest that the conditions under which the dogs are kept were inhumane and unsanitary—in one word, atrocious. This, together with absolutely no quality control in the breeding, and then the consequent stresses of crating and shipping very young puppies to the retail outlets, makes of this whole business one of the most sickening forms of the commercial exploitation of animals. Often the stores charge prices for inferior quality pups that a local breeder wouldn't dream of asking; you can often get a purebred quality pup for half the price from a private breeder. So I urge everyone to avoid buying a pet from a large retail store unless you can ascertain that the animal came from a local breeder. Better still, find a local breeder yourself through the pet column of your newspaper.

Another inhumane fad, outlawed in England, is ear cropping. Breeds like the Doberman pinscher, Great Dane, and schnauzer commonly have this operation performed at a psychologically critical age in their lives. The operation is itself extremely painful and postoperative care, including splinting the ears, which often become infected, is both cruel and barbaric. Some dogs are permanently head-shy after this early trauma. Even if it hurts only a little, why do it at all? The animal's suffering is an unnecessary human indulgence which, unlike neutering and declawing, doesn't make the animal a better pet.

Suppose you wanted to show your dog and the breed standards call for cropped ears? Or you say the judges in the ring won't look at a dog with uncropped ears? The answer is simple: change the standards and get rid of the judges! After all, people and not Mother Nature decreed such rules!

Before considering other animals, there are other widespread abuses of dogs which, as responsible human beings, we have an obligation to prevent. One is dogfighting. For this illegal but popular rural sport dogs are bred and trained to attack each other for man's vicarious enjoyment and attendant financial gain: betting goes along with killing. Another abuse is attack training. Many "schools," run by unqualified mercenaries, use cruel physical and psychological methods to create a canine psychopath. Ideally, ownership of such animals should be under state or federal control. Owners at least should be required to have full credentials to attest to their abilities to handle such an animal, and the schools ought to be inspected regularly and approved only if they use humane training procedures.

In regard to the mistreatment and abuse of other animals, I believe that we must begin with a firm ethical premise: namely, domestic (farm) and wild animals should be destroyed or otherwise used by man only when it is essential to end suffering or for the essential benefit of mankind. By the essential benefit of man I mean the killing required to control certain diseases or ecological imbalances and in order to provide food and other animal by-products that we require for subsistence. Much exploitation of animals falls into the luxury category—sport hunting or trapping or raising animals in captivity for their fur—a commodity used more frequently out of vanity than simply to keep warm.

If a woman could feel the pain and terror of the wild animals who died so that she could wear their fur—American lynx, beaver, bobcat, wolverine, fox, raccoon and countless other varieties—the very touch of her coat would make her ill.

I am sure that many people would become vegetarians tomorrow if they were to see the conditions under which cattle and pigs are kept on many large feed lots and intensive factory-farms today. Vegetable protein (lentils, beans, soya, etc.) is no less nutritious, and can be produced more economically, than beef or pork.

What would certainly turn your stomach and change your mind for good would be viewing food animals being slaughtered. Even today—although the practice is much restricted thanks to the intervention of humane organizations (which you can support by joining tomorrow!)—many animals are simply stunned and bled and hacked up while still alive. Ritual kosher slaughter continues this inhumane practice today; and I pity those who eat such meat.

Lipstick, perfumes, and other cosmetics should be of vegetable origin only. Oils and ambergris from whales are used by the cosmetics industry; they support the slaughter of these incredible, beautiful creatures on the verge of extinction and so indirectly does the person who buys such products in ignorance and innocence (you!). Hopefully alternative ingredients will be in wide use soon, before all the whales are gone.

Vegetable and other synthetic substitutes are available; there is no reason, other than vested interest, for the unnecessary destruction of animals to continue.

Musk from animals (especially from the civet cats) is also a major ingredient in perfume. Pause and think how they get the musk: it's like killing a cow every time you milk it. This is an extreme example of what I call nonessential exploitation of animals which we must all learn to recognize. Our survival is intimately linked with theirs, because the earth is delicately balanced, interrelated and interdependent.

Another violent and inhumane nonessential exploitation of animals, either directly or indirectly, which often goes by unrecognized and unchallenged, is in the film industry. Although a dummy shark was used in *Jaws*, other films like the science fiction spoof on rats, *The Shark's Treasure*, and countless other films, including the all-American Western, involve the unnecessary injuring and annihilation of thousands of animals each year. Few in the audience think twice about seeing a few crocodiles, snakes, or sharks killed for their viewing pleasure. There are plenty more you might contend—but unfortunately this old belief is way off the mark: all of nature's resources are finite and we should regard every living thing and "resource" as rare and precious.

An indirect effect of films on animal misuse is not rare, but it is less frequently noticed. The Davy Crockett films resulted in commercial opportunists creating a market for coonskin hats—many made out of kidnaped pet cats, in addition to live-trapped and shot rabbits and raccoons. A large bookstore offered heaps of sharks' jaws for sale as an added attraction following the film release of *Jaws* in order to promote the paperback sales of this and other related books. The shark is not just a useless lethal creature to be exterminated or exploited in shortsighted quick-cash commercial ventures. But few people think twice about such exploitation. Why? Because our culture and values are basically materialistic, so far removed from contact with the natural world.

As we should question the ethics of killing or injuring animals intentionally for entertainment purposes, so too we should question the sport hunter and fisherman. While it may be hard to understand how a man can derive pleasure from killing an animal, nevertheless it is true—and pathetic. Man was once a hunter, and as I emphasize in *Between Animal and Man*, this is one manifestation of the essentially male ego at work. In this particular ego state of consciousness, called humanocentric, all is subservient to man and the world is his to exploit and manipulate as his selfish desires and values dictate. Women's liberation, conservation, and other consciousness-raising movements may help men, and mankind in general, rise above these ignorant and destructive modes of thought and action.

I also abhor the exploitation of animals in zoos and circuses where they are used simply to entertain the public, neglecting the inculcation of a sense of reverence for life and concern for the conservation of such animals in their natural habitats. While most zoos are showing signs of improvement, circuses and roadside menageries are light-years behind. Seeing a man controlling a group of elephants or lions and tigers in the ring may be awe inspiring, but it is another crude illustration of man relentlessly imposing his will on all that should be wild and free. Why should a mountain lion spend its life in a cage instead of on a mountain, or a tiger jump through a hoop of fire and ride on top of a horse instead of prowling the eternal night of its jungle sanctuary, protected from sport hunters and fur traders? It may be better for such animals to be dead than in a zoo or circus; although the former may provide temporary sanctuary until such time as they can be once more released into protected habitats in the wild.

Zoos and circuses I once enjoyed, but knowing what I know now, they only make me sad and frustrated. Like the animals, we too are in a crazy circus of modern life, restricted in our own cages of narrowly defined and self-limiting values and opportunities. The way we treat and relate to animals is, sadly enough, like a mirror reflecting the way in which we treat and relate to our own kind. We have a long way to go before we can rediscover our freedom and kinship with all life: it must first begin, surely, with responsibility and respect.

I see little responsibility and respect for animals apparent in scientific research today. Overexploitation and unnecessary destruction of animals continues under the guise of education, scientific progress, and human safety and health research in high-school science-fair projects, university research laboratories, and commerical drug- and chemical-testing laboratories. Such a tremendous waste of animals, so little respect for life, in the countless experiments which are purely academic games and of little benefit to either animal or man. Using animals to test the potential toxicity of new products is not ethical practice when such products are nonessential luxury items. We don't *need* these things; they

are not essential to our well-being, and such killing is unnecessary and immoral. The only motives are safe production and profit. Much biomedical research could be done
without cats, dogs, and monkeys; laboratory rodents, and
fruit flies, especially bred for such work, tissue culture and
computer simulation are viable alternatives that should be
more widely encouraged.

The longer we remain ignorant and insensitive to abuse,
the more ignorant and insensitive will our relationships become in every case. Surely, the more we demean nature the
more we demean ourselves.

We are, let us hope, mature enough to rise above the cruel vicarious enjoyment of bullfights and cockfights. But are
we strong enough to break traditions of trophy hunting, of
killing for pleasure? Are we responsible enough to deplore
the commercial exploitation of animals in the manufacture
of nonessential consumer products? Can we always be alert
to recognize violations of man's dominion over animals—
which should be a stewardship—when these are being perpetrated?

We must be mature, strong, responsible, and alert, for in
the humane ethic and salvation of animals is our own salvation. Our future and theirs is inseparable.

Killer Dogs in Fact and Fiction

Best-seller pulp trade novels have gone from bad to
worse; from supersleuth human killers in *The Day of the
Jackal* and *The Dogs of War* to "real" animal killer horrors
in *Jaws* and *The Dogs*. Most have been or will be made into
movies. What does this trend mean? What values, needs,
and feelings do such "entertaining" materials reflect in our
society?

A former student of mine, now a Hollywood screenwriter, recently consulted me on the approach he should take
vis à vis one of these man/science-created killer-dog novels
in adapting it for film. I suggested that he make a film of
Olaf Stapeldon's *Sirius*, written in 1944, a most sensitive

story about a mutant dog—the mutation giving the dog intelligence on a human level. In contrast, today's stories are crass, sensationalistic, and basically insensitive to animal intelligence and emotions. The emphasis, which sells, is on violence and human fear, if not on sex. The salient part of my letter to this screenwriter went as follows:

> I met Robert Calder, author of *The Dogs*, on a television talk show. He is out to make money, naturally, and was a little apologetic with me about his book. My general philosophy is that animals, ideally, should be used as teachers or examples to reconnect us with nature and to bring out some of the better qualities of human beings. To focus upon violence as in *Jaws*, and human-created violence in dog mutants as in *The Dogs* is not, I believe, what people need today. A greater reverence for life and understanding, what I call the animal/nature connection, needs to be re-established.
>
> However, *The Dogs* and other sensationalistic pulp (reflecting what some say the public wants) may be significant of the following: we are becoming increasingly fearful and paranoid about what happens when we change the natural order, including the environmental and genetic structure of animals. The division between what was even recently considered far-out science fiction and scientific possibilities is shrinking, so that today *The Dogs* is within the realm of possibility. As such, it could be construed as a warning to us not to interfere with the natural order any more. This could eventually reach the proportions of a paranoid antiscience reminiscent of the Middle Ages; and, indeed, there are countless examples of man's dominionistic meddling with nature backfiring with serious consequences. If *The Dogs* were used as a sensational but educational kind of warning, I would be happy to become involved as a program consultant.
>
> I do believe, however, that people could do with a little inspiration. For many Olaf Stapledon's book *Sirius*, about a modern dog with human intelligence, is a far superior, more entertaining and more sensitive kind of book that could have a much more positive impact on the television viewing audience during prime time.

As author, veterinarian and psychologist, I am interested in what books and films, especially those concerning animals, hit the popular fancy and what their popularity may reflect. I see in the violence and supernormal and supernatural powers in the mass media entertainment, and in the voluminous publications concerning the occult, symptoms of the growing fear in the populace of out-of-control change. Genetic engineering and the creation of potentially lethal new life forms, or nuclear power plant radiation and pollution, pose very real problems, which call for serious study, not blind panic.

In the Middle Ages, mankind feared the "unknown" forces of nature; the plague (black death) ravaged Europe. Demons and evil monsters flourished in mythology and folklore. Many people turned to religion as an escape or for salvation, while others turned to witchcraft and other occult practices; these commonplace devotions were a "power" substitute for the uncertainties of life. Today, a similar fear of the unknown, uncontrollable forces of nature—those causing earthquakes, droughts, famine, a possible new ice age—and of the consequences of our ignorant tampering with the world—pollution and cancer—herald a return to the "Dark Ages." Man-induced (environmentally caused) cancer ravages one in every four of the populace today, and is analogous to the black death of the Middle Ages. A man-made killer dog, by analogy, is no different.

In many ways, our modern technological civilization is regressing to this dark age. The cycle is repeating itself. More and more people today are turning back to religion, to witchcraft and other occult practices, and to Eastern philosophies in search of salvation and security; the religion of science seems to have created both real and imaginary monsters instead of saving us. Science does not seem to hold the answers to save us from ourselves, as the church had no direct way of saving our ancestors from themselves and from the black death.

Free-roaming packs of superintelligent killer dogs? Such a tale of science backfiring is not only within the realm of possibility, it is acceptable (and financially successful) because people *are* afraid of the backlash of man-made mistakes, be they human Frankensteins or canine "Caldersteins." Fears are affirmed and justified by such tales.

Caught in a vortex of chaotic insecurity, we play with our fears, and enjoy fantasies of death, of global annihilation, of violence, of humanocidal forces in nature—killer sharks and dogs. The unpredictable and uncontrollable forces of nature seem not only beyond our control, but beyond any understanding.

What does it all mean? Is it that we are afraid of ourselves and of our own creations and actions that seem to have a way of backfiring? The cancer-creating DDT we sprayed on insects on our corn is now in the fish we eat and in the breasts of mothers who nurse the next generation.

What I am afraid of is that people won't see themselves in the mirror, but will blame nature, refusing to take the responsibility for their own actions and arrogant irresponsibility. As for *Jaws*, and killer grizzly bears, dogs, and wolves—even giant killer rabbits and bees!—they are basically illusory projections of our own minds abetted by inventive but misguided writers. We should be afraid of ourselves and not of nature. We should recognize the need to have dominion over ourselves, and not over nature and all creatures great and small.

Much of our Western mythos concerning animals is negative. And this is aggravated by ignorance of the true nature of our animal kin—basically nonviolent, sensitive, feeling; even intelligent and loving. The wolf, for example, is still regarded by many as a savage, sly, and blood-lusting killer; the grizzly bear is little better regarded. Whales are just big dumb "fish" to be rendered into oil. The mountain lion is a cunning killer of children and helpless livestock; like all predators, it should be exterminated, some would say. Domestic animals—cattle, pigs, poultry—are dumb and stupid, so they cannot possibly suffer in the crowded confinement of factory-farms. Monkeys and rats, dogs and rabbits, don't feel pain as we do, it is claimed, and don't have "real" emotion, so it is safe to perform all kinds of painful experiments upon them without harming them physically or psychologically. We demean ourselves through such ignorance and indifference, inhumanity and insensitivity.

The negative mythos concerning animals in our culture is widespread and makes America stand out from all nations. We are the most technologically advanced nation, and yet the advancement is in sharp and ironic contrast to the way in which we regard and treat animals. Here we live still in the dark ages of ignorance, negative mythos, and indifference. But the tide is slowly changing for the better—though no thanks to books like *Jaws* and *The Dogs*. Will we never, as in *Beauty and the Beast*, transcend our illusory fears with compassion, love, and understanding? I would like to write and play the title role in the next Hollywood Wolfman feature. For surely, when man and beast are united as one, we become gods. Yet as I emphasize in *Between Animal and Man*, we are a long way from such a dream (of the Sagittarian age).

Compare our westernized negative view of animals with any native culture. The American Indian animal mythology is rich in *positive* animal attributes (they are seen as little people, as cousins, brother and sisters) and their mythos is balanced with a sound logos: a knowledge of the role and value of all life in the balance of nature, in the great hoop of life.

Utilitarian values contaminate our relationship with animals. People "use" dogs for many purposes: in attack work, as working dogs, for status, for research, and for other purely utilitarian purposes. But surely their ultimate and highest "use" is to help us become more human; that is, more humane, compassionate, responsible, and understanding. As I emphasized in *Between Animal and Man*, we must become the stewards of creation. Nature gains its ultimate expression in consciousness through mankind.

We sink into near unconsciousness, into a subhuman and subanimal level of awareness, when we play with or indulge our imaginary fears, as in creating "monster" dogs. We

sink into ignorance when we distort reality and can no longer recognize the truth beneath the illusory surface of the
monster: the truth that animals are not like that (but with
one exception perhaps—the human animal). I abhor the
felling of trees to make paper to publish crass books that
demean animals by making them into Frankenstein monsters. We forget that the original story of Frankenstein was
sensitive and tragic, like *Sirius*, not violent and malevolent.

What of the effects of positive and negative press and of
such books and films on animals and of certain dog breeds?
Positive press nurtures appreciation, humane treatment,
and conservation of wild species. Negative press and the
negative, demeaning animal mythos of adult and children's
stories leads to justification of the destruction of brother
wolf, grizzly bear, or coyote on sight. (If you *must* read *Little Red Riding Hood* to your child, say that it is unreal, but
fun; then read a true story about wolves, like my book *The
Wolf*.)

Too much unreal positive press, like the impossible Lassie, can set up unreal expectations. A lady called me recently—she no longer liked her border collie because when she
needed help it didn't respond like Lassie. She was attacked
and the dog just stood by and did not come to her rescue.
However, she had never trained the dog, and was a very
assertive person—no doubt the dog thought she could take
good care of herself! So much for illusory positive preconceptions.

What of the negative with regard to dogs? Consider the
effect of a horror film about killer shepherds or Dobermans.
Someone meeting a friendly "Dobe" the next day will emit
fear and apprehension and these reactions may well confuse the dog. It may even see such reactions as a threat and
growl defensively: this behavior, like a self-fulfilling prophecy, would be interpreted as offensive. Yes, see—they
say—the killer instinct surfaces!

It seems tragic that our closest, most trusting and noble
animal companion, the dog, is being misrepresented and de-

meaned to titillate our fears of some man-created animal intelligence unleashed against its creator; exploited to protect us from our paranoia as an attack-trained guardian.

Human beings once learned stewardship and reverence for life in their early domestication of the dog; in many ways, man created dogs in his own image. (See *Understanding Your Dog.*) Let us look again at our dogs and at what we are doing to them, in fact and in fiction. They have, indeed, become our mirrors, reflecting so much of our actions, feelings, and values. Are they now being created in fact and fiction to reflect our need for power, or for powerful allies? Or are these manifestations more subtle: a reflection of our own fears and anxieties and of our enjoyment of violence and cruelty? We may perhaps see our canine kin clearly and appreciate them fully for what they are only when we see and know ourselves in the mirror of life's experiences.

25

The Human Animal
and Animal Archetypes

THE SHRIKE-VOICED shrew exclaimed, "Snake in the grass, you weasled your way in here and ape around. You really get my goat, you rat fink son of a bitch. You're worse than a bear with a sore tooth, stubborn as a mule, and don't even have horse sense, you swine."

"Cut out the bull, foxy lady," replied the cockscomb with a sheepish grin. "Don't monkey with me, you slothful cow, there's no hope for bird-brained bitches like you."

Lost for words, she hissed, "You beastly beast."

Clearly both have forgotten that they were human.

Or had they? Only human beings can degrade themselves and animals alike. Perhaps the worst insult (for an animal) is to be called a man!

But there are more prophetic truths underlying these negative zoomorphisms. In demeaning ourselves, we demean nature—both humankind and animalkind. Through a twist in our thinking and perceiving, we anthropomorphically project these negative attributes back onto the animal.

Our language, reflecting and often shaping our state of consciousness/awareness, is tainted with these highly charged negative attributes. It is as though any creature that is not helplessly infantile, irresistibly cuddly, gracefully "female," or inscrutably aloof (a duckling, koala, deer,

and lion or eagle respectively), is going to evoke some negative feeling or reaction.

Even humorous or more positive statements about animals are usually anthropomorphic: tight as a tick, crazy as a
loon, loyal as a dog, proud as a lion, wise as an owl, and so
on.

For me all this implies how our language, our enculturat-
ed ways of thinking and perceiving in relation to the natural
world, are extremely biased; overhearing comments between adults and between parents and children at zoos
confirms this. There is a flaw, a serious defect in the human
mind, and it is simply this: most of the time (in our everyday state of constricted consciousness) we only see the
world in relation to ourselves. Perception is filtered, thinking is twisted, by virtue of the fact that we are usually incapable of seeing the animal as it really is (and, of course, seeing an animal out of its natural context in a zoo cage is no
help either).

I believe that our minds, or at least the ego,* which
makes us so anthropocentric, prevents us from really seeing others (people and animals alike) and therefore from understanding. The essence of the "thing in itself" is denied
to our understanding.

An easy and often very revealing exercise is a fantasy
game involving animals. Close your eyes, relax, and take a
movie in your mind of the first animal that comes into your

---

*With rare exceptions (such as sponge and coral reef communities and bee and
termite societies) each animal is essentially the center of its own universe: its
nervous system, as a structure for receiving and transmitting information, makes
it so. As our nervous systems and society alike become more complex (without
the former, we would resemble ants) a point came in our evolution when we became conscious of our consciousness; we knew that we knew (maybe we didn't
realize quite how much we didn't—and don't—know). Along with this new development came the ego, that part of our minds with which we reflectively define ourselves and the world in which we live. It has served its purpose and we are now
evolving, hopefully, toward the next stage of a collective consciousness; the age
of the individual (ego) is drawing to a close and a true humanity, with a global
sense of unity with all human—and animal—kind is emerging. *One Earth, One
Mind* is the title of one of my forthcoming books on this phenomenon and the contemporary problems that we face today at the destructive and exploitative immature level of ego and egosphere.

head. After a while, instructions are given to go somewhere else and find another, very different animal: this is "filmed" like the first one and all its movements, feelings and thoughts are similarly recorded. Finally, the two different animals are put together in the same scene and their feelings and reactions toward each other are recorded.

This exercise is usually rewarding for participants because the animals they choose are often projections of one or more facets of their own personalities (sometimes in conflict), which may be revealed when the two are "filmed" together. In giving the animal actors feelings and thoughts, the projection-identification is assured at the onset. Participants are often astounded at the appropriateness of the animals that some people choose for themselves: a shy chipmunk, a clumsy bear, a powerful cougar, a free and happy dolphin, a homely dog, and so on. Sometimes the animal archetype they choose is quite different from what others might anticipate: an angry lion concealed in a passive person, a wild, free eagle in an overly cautious and inhibited person.

Another exercise that can be done before participants share their "mind movies" is to have everyone give the two animals names that best fit each person in the group's personality and ways of relating to the group. The people who are most themselves with others often have the same animals in their fantasy script as are ascribed to them by other participants!

A cat, by virtue of its subtle almost noncommunicativeness and its strong independence and inner-directedness, is not the pet for many seeking a companion animal. They would prefer a more demonstrative, "accessible" and controllable dog. Others appreciate the cat for what it is—no clinging vine like so many other-directed, overdependent dogs. Because of the cat's apparent aloofness, a mystique, somewhat analogous to the feminine mystique, has grown around it; unfathomable, inscrutable; and like a woman, the more distant and aloof, the more alluring to the male ego. Being distant and hard to reach is one way of controlling and dominating others; for some people, it is an effective defense mechanism.

So many animal myths, and attitudes toward animals and people (including women) in general, are contaminated by such unfounded projections of the human imagination (or male ego). That which we do not understand creates uncertainty, anxiety, and apprehension. The void is filled in with rationalizations and mythical fabrications which prevent us from seeing and appreciating the cat (or the woman or whatever) for itself. The "aloof" cat (or woman) might simply be afraid of you, or put off by your obvious apprehension—your expectations may be self-fulfilling!

I have been perplexed by my own and other people's reactions to some animals that we tend to categorize as male or female. A deer is always a "she," a wolf or wild dog a "he." Apart from the "female" mystique of a "distant" cat or a graceful panther, this general categorization I believe reflects not an archetypal projection but something more subtle and ineffable: it may be related to a kind of energy field, which may be negative (drawing in the environment) or positive (penetrating the environment).

A female receives, takes in, while a male penetrates. This is a perceptual and cognitive style rather than a sexual mode; although the latter mode is part of the phenomenon, it does not, I believe, wholly determine it.

A deer—as representative of any prey species, one that is hunted—always takes in the environment, ready to flee at the sight of danger. The eyes are set well to the sides of the head to provide an almost 360-degree field of vision.

A wolf—as representative of any predator species, one that hunts—penetrates the environment, ready to stalk and attack. The eyes are set close together to provide a narrower, more focused penetrating, rather than scanning-absorbing, view of the world.

These extreme differences in structure and behavior are not so clear-cut in men and women—but my wolves tell me that they may well exist. Most wolves that I have hand raised are usually afraid of men, but not of women or children. Children are always "taking in" the environment, a natural aspect of their curiosity. Adults are more stimulus bound, more focused in their behavior; they fixate, attend, and "penetrate," especially with their eyes. A direct stare to a wolf, to any animal, is intimidating and may provoke a defensive reaction.

Women, with my wolves, tend to be passively accepting ("Come to me and we will be friends") while men are generally more assertive/insertive ("I will make friends with you").

Early in our own evolution, men were the hunters (the wolves) and the women the plant-gatherers (the deer), mothers and homemakers.

From this division of labor, physical and psychological differences evolved between male and female—however, not to the degree that roles cannot be reversed: a deer may still attack a wolf and a wolf may flee. There also evolved a difference in the way men and women perceive and interact with the environment, having as a result negative and positive energy fields respectively. Of course the charge of polarity may be reversed, but I believe that the resting or steady state energy potentials of male and female are complementary opposites. This is what my wolves may have been telling me in their reactions. It's nothing new: the Ying/Yang of male and female opposites has been recognized for millennia by the wise ancients who were probably more in touch with the real world than we are today in our unreal, unseeing world of intruding thoughts, expectations, and projections.

It is these energy fields that change with emotions, thoughts, and physical and mental disease. Their balance and harmony are maintained by right feeling, thinking, living, and relating, but we know little of these things in Western medicine, since we have been preoccupied with studying disease and do not fully understand the dynamics of health (which is something more than the simplistic medical definition of health being the absence of disease!).

Subtle differences in these energy fields probably under-

The wolf, creature of myth and legend—and an archetype of deeply ingrained significance in all cultures—still is persecuted by man in ignorance of its true nature.

lie the authenticated feats of psychic trailing in animals that find their owners although they have moved (sometimes hundreds of miles away).

With animals and people, we react before we have time to see, to appreciate, and to know. Reactions are based upon *preconceptions* or expectations (he, she, or it may be dangerous or is not to be trusted), *emotional needs* (you must protect, cuddle, or care for him, her, or it) and *projections* (the hawk or lion appeals to your wild spirit or your desire for freedom and power or status). A fourth reaction is the *projected rejection*, where you turn off if you see in others qualities that you don't like in yourself (an obese and "greedy" pig or a scabrous "cowardly" hyena).

If we accepted our own flaws and weaknesses and had more self-respect, surely we could accept and respect others for what they are—no matter what race, breed, color, or form they assume.

Are those slimy green iridescent blobs with hairy tentacles in their flying saucers aware of this? Man is still an alien to himself and to the world as a whole; he is not yet ready to experience an alien being. He is not yet fully human; the name he gave himself, *Homo sapiens*, is arrogantly premature. How many of us could relate to an alien life form of probably superior intelligence (and the sensitivity that goes with it), and not react in the habitual ways alluded to earlier?

If we are not able to see, nor in many cases even willing to try to see, we are not yet ready to know the secrets of the universe—in other words, ourselves.

Animals, I think, can help us in this regard. Our biological kinship with all life, by a simple but radical change in thinking and perceiving, can be transmuted into a conscious reverence for all life, for all creatures great and small—beautiful, ugly, worthless, valuable, venomous.

I have likened the mongrel dog to the flexible, infinitely adaptable Renaissance man and "specialist" dogs like bloodhounds to human scientists and technologists who similarly specialize in more or less exclusive use of only one part of their potentialities (biocomputer brains and noses respectively!).

Sometimes related to the reasons people like a particular kind of pet is the common observation that pet and owner often look alike. Fulfilling certain needs is one thing, but resembling each other physically and/or psychologically may be more than coincidence—a reciprocal reflection of anthropomorphic and zoomorphic archetypes! Other times the pet may be a projection of an inner archetypal ideal not evident on the surface; a shy man keeps a lion in his backyard, and a fat woman shares her life with a cheetah or saluki.

We are animals, the most complex and evolved; being evolved from them, we have carried with us many of their qualities, both structural and behavioral. In fact the more I study man, the more "polymorphous," or protean in nature, he seems, or at least potentially so.

Another truth arising from this is that if we were to know everything about man (or any other species, for that matter), we would know everything about the world. This evolutionary and ecological fact, recognized for thousands of years in Eastern philosophies such as Zen, implies that everything is interrelated in time and place (earth space).

Logically, therefore, the more human we become, the more aware we will be of these relationships—of the interdependence and interpenetration of everything on earth. Today we are beginning to use computers to monitor the biosphere; it seems an evolutionary inevitability that, with these new developments or extensions of the human mind, we are on the threshold of earth-mind or global consciousness.

But we are not there yet, by any means. How many of us are like those caged animals in the zoo, out of context with the natural world as a whole, or overcivilized and dependent, like so many of our domesticated animals? Trapped in a city jungle or a suburban dormitory, distracted, ungrounded, we can lose contact with the earth and ourselves alike. People (or animals) *are* their environments—a sick, polluted environment, or one lacking in diversity and *organic reality*, will cause physical and mental sickness. This is as true for captive zoo animals as it is for farm livestock, household pets, and people. Man and his environment are inseparable; if he injures, destroys, or drastically modifies it, he cannot avoid the consequences to his own psychophysical well-being. Healthy environments make for healthy animals and people, and vice versa—a fact forgotten by Western medicine, lost in technological "progress" and the complexities of the individual—which they will never understand or really help until they see man in the context of his environment. We don't need doctors—we need a healthy physical and social environment.

During the Second World War, some zoos in Europe were bombed, and cages were sometimes torn apart. Some animals escaped, but many others preferred to stay in the "safety" of their cages.

People are like that, too. They adapt (to a pathogenic "caged" way of life) or compromise ("At least I've got security"), but many are too afraid and most don't know where to go, how to get there, or what to do when they arrive.

I envisage no Shangri-la, but simple communities where one can be human, where we design with nature: where a toad is a toad and man is a man, equally revered and free to be as their natures incline them—each developing toward the fulfillment of its being, and relatedness to all. The archetype of "man" would have no negative connotations, since man would be wholly animal and human, something which today he is far from being. And with this integration of man and nature, animals, both wild and domestic, would take on a new and deeper significance (as emphasized in chapter 11). Pets and other animals can help us see part of ourselves often hidden from us because of our habitual ways of thinking and perceiving. If we can receive their "message," then what I have said will not be simply an optimist's dream. People would become responsible stewards and share concern and reverence for all life.

Animals can make us more human!

Conclusions:

Animal Rights and Humane Alternatives

I SPEND MUCH of my time answering phone calls and letters from pet owners, humane society officials, and veterinary colleagues concerning many and varied pet problems. Although I don't always welcome the burden of extra work some days, I have benefited greatly, gaining much insight and knowledge from these "extras." This, together with what I have learned from my own extensive research on normal and abnormal behavior in animals, has been incorporated into this book, along with additional observations from scientific colleagues where relevant.

The pet phenomenon, as a multi-billion-dollar market, attracts big business corporations, ethical and unethical, good and bad products and practices, from companies that say dogs need an all-meat diet to puppy mills that mass produce animals like wholesale potatoes. Materialism and crass commercialism exploits and violates the relationship not only between the "consumer" and pet, but between man and man, and man and nature.

I believe that above and beyond all the reasons for owning a pet and all the needs a pet can fulfill, another level of relationship and of experiencing exists: to understand and appreciate the pet for itself. To know that it has many needs and feelings much like our own is a first step. Empathy and understanding, rather than emotional, sentimental anthropomorphization, are the key to unconditional love, to a dependency-free, nonmanipulative or nonexploitative relationship. Tied in with reverence for all life is self-acceptance; our pets can help us understand ourselves since they mirror so many of our virtues and weaknesses: virtues of loyalty and unconditional affection, weaknesses of jealousy, possessiveness, and overdependency.

All of life is a learning experience, and our pets can add depth and enrichment to our lives when we are able to see and to know. We cease to learn, and to live, when our eyes and minds are closed. This book, I hope, has helped you get closer to understanding your pet and to knowing yourself as well. If it has given you some insight into seeing and appreciating the animal for itself, I know that your relationship with animals and people alike will improve, since you will be in touch with some of their virtues and weaknesses, and with your own as well.

But pets are not the only creatures in our lives. Many others fall within the scope of our moral concern, and we owe an enormous debt to them. There are those which provide us with food—meat, milk, and eggs—and those used to test consumer products, including pharmaceuticals, cosmetics, and household expendables. Others are used in biomedical research and in teaching.

One of the reasons I joined the Humane Society of the United States, a nonprofit national organization funded by private donations, is to work for animal rights. Animal welfare is not yet fully guaranteed either by existing laws or by the awareness and ethical responsibility of those who are in charge of either making the laws or caring for the animals. The range of abuse and unethical exploitation is extensive, a summary of which is listed in the following table.

(Note: This table is by no means complete, but it does demonstrate that most animal uses fall in the categories of entertainment and exploitation.)

SUMMARY TABLE OF NONESSENTIAL USES AND ABUSES OF ANIMALS

Biomedical Research

Much repetition and
irrelevant research

High-school and college
teaching projects.

Scientific collecting–
some native and imported
species (especially
primates) becoming
endangered.

Testing cosmetics and
other non-essential
market products.

Military "research"

Management/Exploitation

Trapping and fur trade
Whaling
Sealing
Predator "control"
"Factory" farming
Cosmetics industry
  and other non-
  essential animal
  products.
Fur ranches
Mustang roundups
Military use (dolphins)
Introduced alien species
  (and escapes) e.g.
  placing wrong species
  in the wrong environ-
  ment.

Sport/Entertainment

Trophy hunting
Deep sea "trophy" angling
Sport hunting
Ranch-raised game

Horse racing
Rodeos

Greyhound racing
Greyhound training
(with live rabbits)

Bullfighting
Cockfighting
Dogfighting

Roadside zoos
Movie industry and television

Pet Trade

"Puppy mills"
"Exotic" imports
Noneducational
  menagerie collectors
  and traders
Ear cropping

More generalized ecosystem effects to be considered in conjunction with the above include:

Forest mismanagement (clear cutting); pollution of rivers and oceans; effects of excess fertilizers, insecticides, and toxic industrial wastes, oil spills: destruction of habitat by industry, real estate, and agricultural expansion and land development (by construction of dams); inadequate national and international controls on methods of obtaining natural resources—oil, coal, fish, etc., causing extensive damage to ecosystems; impact of diseases from domestic stock and overgrazing on wildlife, etc.

Our technological society urgently needs fossil fuels. It is a top government priority and has now taken precedence over emission control on automobiles and its benefits to public health. The demands of conservationists to stop strip-mining, further desecration of the wilderness, extinction of species, pollution, and depletion of natural resources are contrary to these immediate needs and priorities. They are also contrary to the values of a "progressive" society in which growth is equated with progress. Within this value system, the cancerous nature of such growth cannot be seen, no matter how hard the conservationists may try to make others see. What is needed is a metamorphosis, a change in the perceptions and conceptions of persons locked into a narrow system of values, many of whom directly control the rape of our biosphere. The less we consume, the less we steal from future generations and the more of the irreplacable natural world, with its rich diversity of life, will be preserved.

It is not a question of who is right or wrong; such value judgments merely cause greater unresolved conflicts, as between the conservationist ("Thou shalt not hunt wolves") and the hunter ("It's my right to shoot what I like"). Both factions should evaluate, not judge, their own position with a view to the whole, since within their own value systems they are both equally right. (There is neither right nor wrong, only the ignorances of those who are tied to their own values and locked into their own separate reality or egosphere.)

The day will come, let us hope, when the consensus reality will be such that a wolf or tree, for example, will be valued in its own right. Alternatives may be sought before destroying a tree in order to clear a road, or for lumber. Rather than fighting others in order to preserve the wolf (because it is esthetically pleasing or a rare species—again, these are value judgments), it may instead be seen in an even broader perspective: as part of an ecological whole, as an intrinsic part, a microcosm of the macrocosm that our minds and scientific knowledge can barely comprehend in relation to the consequences of human interference. We are part of this ecological whole, in both body and spirit, and we are therefore an inseparable part of the tree, the wolf, or any other manifestation of creation.

It will be a different world when a man thinks twice and looks first for an alternative before he dams a river or over-turns a stone, knowing that within the river and beneath the stone are microcosms of life with as much right to live as he. Such reverence for all life will improve the quality of human relationships and of the way in which man interacts with nature. As the steward of planet earth, he must as-sume full responsibility for the consequences of his own in-tervention or inaction, as the case may be.

In animal research, the experimenter should question his own personal motives where animals may be unnecessarily propagated and experimented upon. Are the experiments simply being conducted in order to generate publications (publish or perish), are they needlessly repetitive insofar as teaching purposes require, or simply designed to develop some new nonessential consumer product?

Objective and scientific detachment can lead to loss of reverence for life, where subjects become mere numbers for statistical analysis. This detached approach is the reason high school students can contemplate, and then be encouraged to perform, unnecessary and questionable experiments in the name of creative scientific enquiry. Unnecessary, because they have been done before, and questionable because the experiments may involve undue suffering (such as experiments on the effects of scalding on skin healing in hamsters, or skin-grafting in inbred strains of mice referred to me by high school teachers seeking advice on experimental design!).

In livestock husbandry, materialistic values and priorities may take precedence over all else. These values can destroy any reverence or respect for the life forms that are kept like vegetables in fattening stalls or battery cages. Motives of production and profit ultimately override concerns of humane treatment, unless inhumane treatment leads to a drop in production and profits. Modern farming is just like an industry, utilizing the genome of the animal like a machine to convert ingested materials into edible animal protein. Genetic selection may fit the various strains and hybrids to such conditions and, being so modified and adapted, the conditions might not be quite as inhumane as they appear to be on the surface.

Certainly livestock husbandry and especially agriculture, with its multi-acred monocultures of corn, wheat, and potatoes, need a more holistic, ecological renaissance. The land and livestock alike would perhaps be healthier today if we had not been so profit motivated and had not forced them to maximal production. The metabolic problems of a high-yielding dairy cow and the sickness of the overfertilized fields and pastures are the bad fruits of this progress.

The basic rights of animals are inseparable from those of people. More enlightened people will be more responsible stewards of earth once they begin to think and act in harmony with the rights of other human and nonhuman beings. The pitfalls of egocentric perceptions at the materialistic level and of anthropomorphic projections at the emotional level must be overcome. The dynamic interplay, be it between pet and owner or mankind and nature, would then be appreciated in a different light. The experience of living and of relating would be greatly enriched and illuminated with a deeper significance. The following notes are respectfully

A battery of egg chickens on a modern factory farm, suffering in overcrowded cages.

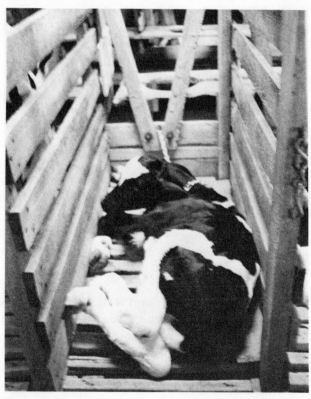

Veal calves are fattened in narrow crates until slaughter, are kept in darkness for 20 to 22 hours a day, and are always chained—a modern, "progressive" farm.

offered as a guide to a more humane and ecologically balanced life-style.

The Food We Eat

Modern intensive farming systems are inhumane, especially for veal calves and to a slightly lesser extent for pigs, poultry, and battery-egg-laying hens. Eat *no* veal or calf liver and eat *less* pork, bacon, chicken, and eggs (unless they are guaranteed to come from free-range hens). Then there will be less suffering. Balance your diet and improve your health with high protein vegetables—lentils, beans, soya— and more fresh vegetables, grains, and fruit in season. Cheese, yogurt, and other dairy products are generally acceptable since most dairy herds are not kept under inhumane, intensive conditions. Eating fish as an alternative is also a valid option for some people.

Avoid tuna until the fishing industry does more to reduce the destruction of dolphins. Eat no imported goose liver (pâté de fois gras) or turtle; the geese are inhumanely force-fed and turtles are becoming endangered through overharvesting.

These dietary decisions are personal of course, and vegetarianism for some is too difficult. I would advocate non-vegetarians to at least become "conscientious omnivores," aware of what they eat.

The Products We Consume

Stick to old (tried, true, and tested) brands, especially of toiletries, household cleaning agents, and nonprescription drugs (particularly eye and mouth washes). "New and improved" products and product development to corner the consumer market with novel but nonessential innovation involve countless animal lives, and often unjustifiable pain and suffering in the course of running safety tests for the consumer. Sticking to the old brands will help reduce industry's incentive to use and abuse more animals in researching and developing more new nonessential products.   · ·

Perfumes should contain no musk (from wild civet cats and other mammals) or ambergris (from whales). Cosmetics labeled as being of vegetable origin will not contain the oil of turtle, or whale or other animal extracts, which the label on the bottle will not usually disclose. Watch also for whale-oil lubricants and mink-oil products.

Clothes and Objects

The smaller your wardrobe, the less energy you will have consumed: cotton and wool are more economical than synthetic (polyester) materials. Kapok and other synthetic fibres are more "humane" insulators of parkas than duck and goose down. Wear no wild animal furs, even if the animal is not on the "endangered" list; these are inhumanely caught and their use for personal decoration alone is ethically untenable. On the basis of this latter point, all ranch-raised furs should be avoided also. Woolen sweaters and Kapok-filled jackets and parkas will keep you just as warm!

Art objects and personal accoutrements may be made from wild animal products—avoid them, since to purchase such objects is to support the needless killing of animals. Avoid art objects and other things made from butterflies, bird's feathers, snake and other animal skins, alligator and ostrich products, sealskin, elephant and walrus ivory, and tortoiseshell (statues, chess sets, jewelry, etc.). Alternative materials are abundant and attractive.

The Shows and Sports We Enjoy

Be on the lookout for TV shows and films, adult and children's books that abuse or demean our animal kin. Voice complaints to the TV networks and their sponsors, local movie houses, bookstores, and public and school libraries. Media materials that create or perpetuate false or negative myths and attitudes toward animals and that detract from the humane ethic of animal rights should be protested against and boycotted. Dog- and cockfight "entertainments," greased-pig catching, bullfights, raccoon baiting, and fox hunting are inhumane and should be boycotted and protested against. Also, because conditions are such that animal abuses are frequent and often unavoidable, horse racing and grayhound racing (which in many states involves prior training with live rabbits and cats) are ethically unacceptable. Other "sports," including trophy and big-game hunting, hunting with bow and arrow, and trophy (deep-sea) fishing, are to be condemned. Hunting as a nonsubsistence activity is ethically and ecologically untenable. Roadside zoos, some municipal zoos, and circuses with various animal acts demand rigorous scrutiny. Alternatives and substitutes are many: soccer, baseball, football for the spectator; nature photography and natural-history study for the hunter/killer; and roulette or backgammon for the gambler!

House and Garden

Avoid using nonselective pesticides and herbicides: they kill indiscriminately, innocent creatures as well as pests and weeds, and they may kill or harm you or your children. Turning lights off on the patio will keep bugs away, as will personal bug repellents. Don't use bug sprays or electric bug "roasters": only a few of the millions you kill would have bitten you and some insects are useful or necessary in the many natural cycles. If you have a big lawn let some part go to seed and create a meadow for butterflies and other insects, for birds and reptiles: and you will provide in this manner (at no cost!) seeds for the birds and small rodents during the winter. And the more energy you can conserve, the fewer goods you buy, and the less meat you use,

Rabbits in restraining stocks are used in many studies, especially in the safety testing of new cosmetics and household chemicals. One inhumane test is the Draize eye test, in which irritants of various concentrations are placed in the rabbits' eyes, causing severe pain.

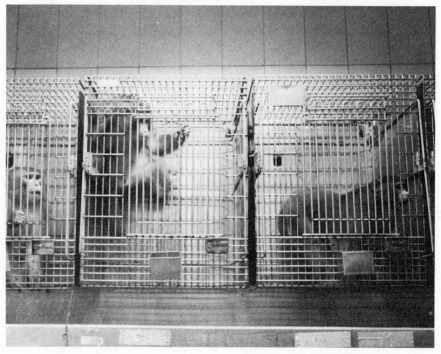

Animals used in research are often kept under extreme conditions of confinement in modern laboratories.

the more energy there will be available for the rest of the world—for countries less affluent—and less damage will be done to areas where the wildlife is threatened by strip-mining, oil spills, deforestation, hydroelectric dam construction, and pollution.

The Animals We Enjoy

Before you obtain a pet—be it dog, cat, gerbil, parakeet or whatever—read up first on how to care for it. You may discover that your life-style is not compatible with keeping a dog or your home not right for a new cat or other pet. (Several helpful pamphlets are available from The Humane Society of the United States, 2100 L Street NW, Washington, D.C. 20037. For a detailed, practical, and philosophical review, see my *Between Animal and Man*.)

As far as wild creatures are concerned, do not purchase them, in a pet store or anywhere!—even those that have been imported or raised in captivity. To sell wild animals as "pets" is a gross misrepresentation (I think it should be labeled fraud). Any life form taken from the wild for study or enjoyment should be returned as soon as possible to the same place in the same condition in which it was found (or better).

Unfortunately, it is a long way, as I see it, before humans will cease to exploit, manipulate, and control wild or domestic animals, other people, or pristine wilderness and ocean. The weakness of humanity is our blindness, a cultural blind spot, which some call ignorance, where a selfish and immature ego claims the world as its own and prevents us from seeing ourselves as a part of the world. Kinship with all life is a biological, evolutionary fact, but our culture, our ways of doing, perceiving, and relating blind us to this reality, and to the spiritual union of all living things which only we, as stewards of planet earth, can express in an ethic of reverence for all life. A mere shift in the way we see and relate can change the world—because as a man sees, so he is. A pet animal can catalyze such awareness, and my book, working through animal, man, and their inter-relationship has, I hope, helped in this direction.

I hope you will begin your first steps along this road immediately after setting this book aside.

Suggestions for Further Reading

Boone, J.A. (1953) *Kinship With All Life*. New York: Harper & Row.

Fox, M.W. (1974) *Understanding Your Cat*. New York: Coward, McCann & Geoghegan.

Fox, M.W. (1972) *Understanding Your Dog*. New York: Coward, McCann & Geoghegan.

Fox, M.W. (1976) *Between Animal and Man*. New York: Coward, McCann & Geoghegan.

Hall, E.T. (1966) *The Hidden Dimension*. New York: Doubleday.

Lorenz, K. (1952) *King Solomon's Ring*. New York: Crowell.

Stapledon, O. (1944) *Sirius*. New York: Penguin.

Index